The 30
Most Common Problems
in Management
and
How to Solve Them

The
30
Most Common
Problems
in Management
and
How to Solve
Them

WILLIAM A. DELANEY

A Division of
American Management Associations

Library of Congress Cataloging in Publication Data

Delaney, William A.
  The 30 most common problems in management—and how to
solve them.

  Includes index.
  1. Problem solving. 2. Management. I. Title.
II. Title: Thirty most common problems in management
and how to solve them.
HD30.29.D44   658   81-69375
ISBN 0-8144-5536-0   AACR2

First Printing

Preface

This book is directed to those who have chosen careers that have led—or will eventually lead—to their managing other people in small or large groups. There is no sure road to success. There are so many variations in people, places, timing, and situations that what works well for you may not work for anyone else, and vice versa. Moreover, what works for you once may not work a second or third time, because you may fail to note some small variation in personal characteristics or circumstances.

This book deals primarily with people—how to work with them, how to manage and motivate them, and how to predict their performance. Whatever you do and wherever you work, you will have to deal with people—and people are unpredictable. Risks and uncertainties are associated with human behavior. Still, people successfully plan and direct projects of great scope and complexity to successful conclusions. They deal with other people successfully or unsuccessfully and, one way or another, they get the job done.

In 25 years of dealing with people at various levels of management and in various organizations, I have made my share of mistakes and have learned from most of them. In addition, I have talked with a number of my colleagues over the years and have learned from them as well. Each chapter in this book deals with a specific problem and how

I have handled it, whether successfully or unsuccessfully. I have included a number of real-life situations.

The person on the way up the ladder has a good technical grasp of the job, but why do some keep going up and some stop early on or in mid-career? Could it be for lack of proper consideration of things other than the day-to-day technical performance on the job?

Many people are willing and able to help you advance your career, if only you take the time to seek them out and ask for their assistance. Most good managers are receptive to requests for information and advice from a subordinate who wants to work hard to advance his or her career. Managers can and will help you.

Generally it is up to you to initiate requests for assistance. Unsolicited help in career advancement is rarely offered because others are unaware of your interest in or desire for such information.

I was well into mid-career before it occurred to me to seek out senior people and ask for their advice. The results were overwhelming. These people responded without exception in such a manner that I gained a wealth of information to help accelerate my career advancement. Some of these people became close personal friends whose association I prize to this day. It was all there for the asking. I wish that I had approached them 10 to 15 years earlier. They weren't aloof at all. They were very understanding and helpful.

This book opens with a survey of the attitudes and habits of some highly successful people. If you find yourself in general agreement with the survey results, perhaps you are a potential top executive.

It seems that those who eventually reach the upper rungs of the corporate ladder work more for personal than social motives. This factor seems to determine how people work and react on a day-to-day basis and how well they do financially. This is not to say that working for nonpersonal or social goals is bad. You set your own goals and priorities and then try to achieve whatever you want from your career. Neither is it true that people who work for personal goals are selfish. Some are very generous and considerate of others. They just separate, in their minds, their reasons for working and their social or charitable activities.

You may note that the same or similar points appear in more than one chapter. This is partly for emphasis and partly because the same cause can have several different effects. Also, because you may want to consider only one problem at a time, I have attempted to make each chapter self-contained. You will find little management theory here. The emphasis is upon applying management principles in a pragmatic manner to real-life situations.

Solutions here have worked well for me and for other managers with whom I have close personal and professional relationships. There are, I am sure, many other ways to meet and handle similar situations and problems. It is hoped that the reader will benefit from my mistakes and experience and move ahead faster and easier as a result.

Some of the topics, such as motivation, communication, and morale, are of daily concern to any manager or aspiring manager. Others, such as layoffs, dismissals, resignations, and politics, do not arise every day. Nevertheless, they can have a severe impact on a person's career and you may not be prepared to deal with situations that do not come up every day.

If the reader can refer to a similar situation and possible solution before, not during or after, the encounter and benefit thereby, then this book will have achieved its purpose.

William A. Delaney

Contents

x Contents

A Survey:
How Top Executives
See Themselves and Others

How far high failure overleaps the bounds of low success.
—*Sir Lewis Morris*

Interest, curiosity, and speculation concerning the top executives in all organizations are common among employees. Wherever we work, or whatever we do, we catch glimpses of these people as they pass by in the office or plant or drive by in their automobiles.

We rarely get to meet them and almost never get to know them as people. What are they like? Are they super beings? How do they earn $100,000 or more a year? What do they do? Are they different from the average person in some strange way that caused them to rise to the top? Can they be categorized in some general way? Is each so unusual that there is no way to study or observe characteristics that may be common to others in like positions? Can we collect data from a sample of such people and possibly identify some behavior or personality patterns that can be used in some way in the never ending search for future leaders? What do these top people think about those who spend their entire careers working under their direction? How are leaders motivated?

These and many other questions concerning leaders have occurred to me as well as to many others. I thought one way to get some answers would be to "ask the person who is one."

I made up a questionnaire and sent out 97 copies to top

1

management personnel of various organizations in the United States. These were addressed to general managers, vice-presidents, and presidents of large corporations and top executives of small corporations.

From these busy executives I hoped to get a 25% return, but more than 30% of them responded.

Although the random sample is small, some patterns emerge to reveal what high-level corporate executives think about themselves, how they got where they are, and how they feel about others.

The questionnaire follows with the percent response given for each question. At the end of this questionnaire, I will attempt to summarize and discuss the typical executive from the responses received.

QUESTIONNAIRE

1. **While in school, what level student did you consider yourself to be?**

   24% Top-caliber   24% Average
   48% Above average   4% Below average

2. **Did you like school?**

   87% Yes   13% No

3. **Did you find school interesting?**

   87% Yes   13% No

4. **Did your higher education help you directly in achieving your present position?**

   83% Yes   17% No

5. **Do you consider yourself to be a tense person?**

   58% Yes   42% No

6. **Are you interested in sports?**

   92% Yes   8% No

7. **Did you ever participate actively in sports?**

   91% Yes   9% No

8. **Were you good at sports?**

   67% Yes   33% No

9. **Did you engage more in team sports (football, basketball) or more in individual sports (golf, track)?**
   65% Team   35% Individual
10. **As a young man or woman, were you the organizer of activities in your group?**
    63% Yes   37% No
11. **Did you aspire early in life (before 30) to reach a position such as you now have?**
    71% Yes   29% No
12. **Did you get your present position mainly by chance or by planning on your part?**
    58% Planning   42% Chance
13. **What single characteristic given below do you rate as most important in achieving your success? Check one.**
    42% Technical ability and interest in work
    29% Very thorough knowledge of job
    4% Complete devotion to my company
    25% Ability to get along with people
14. **Do you owe your success primarily to your own efforts or did others help you substantially to get where you are today?**
    67% Alone   33% Others
15. **What is your opinion of the "average man"?**
    38% Worthy of high respect
    46% Each is so different, I can't answer
    16% All are much the same, but not like me
    0% A "clod"
16. **Do you make decisions on the basis of your intuition or by careful analysis?**
    42% Intuition   58% Analysis
17. **Before you make an important decision, do you consult others?**
    92% Yes   8% No
18. **Do you usually rely on staff subordinates to collect important information for you?**
    87% Yes   13% No
19. **Do you rely heavily on the same few trusted subordinates or do you vary your staff from time to time?**
    39% Same   61% Vary

20. Do you think you are stubborn?
46%   Yes   54%   No

21. Can you easily admit to making a mistake?
96%   Yes   4%   No

22. Do you think your subordinates like you?
79%   Yes   21%   No

23. Do you care whether your subordinates like you?
63%   Yes   37%   No

24. Do you believe your subordinates respect you?
100%   Yes   0%   No

25. Do you care whether or not your subordinates respect you?
92%   Yes   8%   No

26. Are you ever truly satisfied with any work you have done?
71%   Yes   29%   No

27. Can you usually figure out a better way to do a job you have just completed?
79%   Yes   21%   No

28. How would you rate your disposition?
8%   Easygoing   4%   One way
42%   Reasonable   8%   Hard-nosed
34%   Variable   4%   Very aggressive

29. Can you easily dismiss a subordinate who deserves to be fired?
67%   Yes   33%   No

30. Do you delegate to subordinates all of the work that you possibly can?
71%   Yes   29%   No

31. Do you believe you have more in common with chief executives of other companies (even rival concerns) than you have with your own subordinates?
42%   Yes   58%   No

32. Do you associate more socially with executives from companies other than your own?
46%   Yes   54%   No

33. Would you permit any of your relatives to work in your company?
71%   Yes   29%   No

34. What is your main reason for working at your present position?

50%   Money and security
17%   Ego satisfaction
17%   Desire to benefit others
16%   Other

35. Do you want any other job?
42%   Yes   58%   No

36. Do you believe anyone can be very good at a job he or she doesn't like?
25%   Yes   75%   No

37. What do you consider to be the prime motivation factor in your subordinates?
25%   Money and security
16%   Desire to be accepted and to receive approval of their actions
21%   Desire for acceptance and respect of their peers or subordinates
38%   Desire to make meaningful contributions that satisfy themselves

38. What single factor do you consider most significant in preventing a subordinate from rising higher in your organization? Check one.
65%   Indecisiveness
17%   Can't get along with people
18%   Doesn't know enough
0%   Won't take advice
0%   Takes too many risks
0%   Exceeds his authority

39. Are you looking for your replacement now?
42%   Yes   58%   No
If so, is he or she easy to find?
20%   Yes   80%   No

40. What percent of any group do you consider to be doers?
63%   Less than 10%   8%   Over 50%
29%   25% to 50%

41. Are you looking forward to a well-earned retirement?
63%   Yes   37%   No

42. In your opinion, do most people prefer to be led or to make their own decisions?
88%   To be led   12%   Make own decisions

43. Do you worry a lot about work?
  67%   Yes   33%   No
44. If a conflict arises between your home and your work, does your work usually win out?
  83%   Work   17%   Home
45. Do you spend enough time on outside activities?
  42%   Yes   58%   No
46. If you had it to do all over again, would you do it the same way?
  46%   Yes   54%   No
47. Could you select from the list below one major error you have made in your career? Check one.
  5%   Didn't work hard enough
  0%   Worked too hard
  0%   Took too many bad risks
  0%   Took too much advice from others
  29%   Didn't enjoy myself enough on other things
  33%   Was too timid
  5%   Cared too much about others
  5%   Misplaced trust in others
  23%   Other
48. Have you learned much from others since you completed school?
  96%   Yes   4%   No
49. Do you want your replacement to operate his or her way or to continue your way?
  92%   His way   8%   Your way
50. Do you direct a large business or a small (under $1 million annual sales) business?
  71%   Large   29%   Small

Let's try now to discuss a typical top executive from a review of the answers given plus some speculation and interpretation on my part. My analysis may be subjective and the reader may disagree with my interpretation of the data. I undertook this survey with a preconceived notion of what these executives were like and that may influence my evaluation of the data. Readers should draw their own conclusions from the data.

The responses to questions 1 through 4 are not surprising. The executives liked school, found it interesting, and they were mostly above average or average students.

Many previous studies have shown that high grades in school have little or no relationship to success in later life. As these executives (72%) put themselves predominantly in "above average to average" categories as students and they are rating themselves (we tend to judge ourselves most kindly), they do not seem to be from the "cream of the academic crop."

No test in school can ever measure initiative and desire, and many people don't "come alive" until long after they leave school. They are called late bloomers. Their education, however, helped 83% of them directly in reaching their goals.

A 58% majority consider themselves as tense. This fits a preconceived image of a hard-driving executive. The 42% "no" reply is somewhat of a surprise. I thought it would have been lower.

Questions 6–9 were asked to see how these executives as a group felt about sports. The overwhelming response indicates a lifelong interest and participation in sports. Participation, however, is less than interest. They tended more (65%) toward team sports than individual sports. I should have thought the reverse would be true in that these people tend to be strong individuals.

Responses to question 10, however, show an early indication that they were organizers. A 63% majority said when they were young they organized many of the activities in which they participated. An early interest and ability in directing others may be a clue to potential future executives.

Question 11 shows that 71% of these executives had a

plan or idea early in their careers for themselves and where they wanted to go. Most people tend to work their whole careers with no long- or short-range plans for themselves or their families. This may be important in finding out from junior personnel if they have career plans or goals and what they are doing to achieve them. It appears that those who make plans are in the group from which the top people come later.

Question 12 indicated that most (58%) got to where they are now by execution of their plan, whereas 42% achieved position by a chance occurrence of which they took advantage. It is not surprising that serendipity is part of life, but someone had to be there to observe the chance occurrence and then capitalize upon it at the right time.

Question 13 indicates that these people feel that ability and interest in one's work are primary factors in success. Those who received the questionnaire were predominantly from technical organizations, so this answer is not surprising.

Responses to question 14 reveal that by better than two to one executives believe they owe their success mainly to their own efforts.

The purpose of question 15 was to find out what these top people think of the less successful or the more average man or woman. They hold the average person in rather high regard.

Questions 16–19 were asked to find out how these executives make decisions. Almost half (42%) use an intuitive process rather than careful analysis. This fits in with other studies in which it has been stated that either method is valid. Each one should find out which works better and then use it.

The executives do consult others (92%); they use staff subordinates for collecting information (87%), but they vary this staff (61%) from time to time. The reason for this may be they do not want to become too dependent on the same people for everything, which is a wise policy.

Questions 20–25 were asked to find out what the leaders think about themselves and how they believe others see them.

Approximately half rate themselves as stubborn. One answer received merits special note here. One of the respondents marked out the word stubborn on his questionnaire and wrote in the word *steadfast*. He then said the difference between being steadfast and being stubborn was you are steadfast when you are *right*.

Respondents by an overwhelming margin (96%) say they can easily admit to making a mistake. If half rate themselves as stubborn, the two answers don't seem to fit, but no rules say it all has to be logical.

Leaders believe they are liked and respected by their subordinates, but they prefer to be respected. The only 100% affirmative response was that subordinates respect them.

Questions 26 and 27 reveal that respondents have experienced great satisfaction with certain aspects of their jobs, but 79% usually can figure out better ways to do things. This is a most significant indication. Those who are successful believe that whatever the job it it can be done better.

How they rate their own disposition is interesting (question 28): 76% say they are reasonable to variable in their dispositions. One respondent said, "Be reasonable; do it my way." He rated himself as reasonable.

Most (67%) find it not difficult to dismiss an employee who should be fired. This is a requirement that must be developed. Failure to fire incompetent personnel can disrupt the careers of potential executives as well as reduce efficiency.

Most executives (71%) have learned to delegate work to

others. The accomplishment of tasks through other people rather than by doing it directly yourself is the essence of good management.

Questions 31 and 32 indicate that nearly half of the leaders surveyed believe they have more in common with their counterparts in other companies than with those above or below them in their own organizations. They socialize with these outside executives in about the same proportion as well.

The day of the completely devoted organization man appears to be gone. These executives set high professional standards for themselves and are motivated more from within themselves and by others like them than from company loyalty. This is much like the professional athlete or sports manager who does his best at his job for his own personal rewards and satisfaction. The organization or team he represents doesn't seem to affect his performance much one way or the other.

The aggregate answer to question 33 is surprising. All business schools teach against the heresy of nepotism. Managers have all had it drummed into them, *"don't hire relatives."* Yet, 71% of those responding say they would hire relatives. Maybe we all think our relatives are better than your relatives. If so, we should all know better.

The answers to question 34 indicate that 50% work for money and security and only 17% for ego. Other surveys indicate the same tendency for top management personnel to seek highly personal goals as the primary reason for working. This fits with their attitudes previously discussed in response to questions 31 and 32.

Later on we will see the reasons for which the executives believe their subordinates work. There is a big difference.

Responses to question 35 show that most (58%) are satisfied where they are. Their plan is working. Also, 75% believe one must like one's job in order to be good at it (question 36).

Question 37 concerns what executives believe to be the prime motivating factors in their subordinates. The executives believe that subordinates seek and respond to approval of their actions, praise, group acceptance, and making a contribution rather than primarily seeking money and security. They work more for social than for personal or financial reasons.

My experience tends to correspond to the assessment by these executives. I have seen better response from people at many jobs who were motivated more by approval and a kind word rather than by much higher pay, better positions, or job security.

It appears that future management personnel come more from those who early in their careers indicate no basic need for approval from others. They are motivated from within and will do good work when they find an organization whose interests and goals coincide with their own, and they will leave the organization when these interests change. They can stand alone. They do not require support from peer groups.

It follows then that in searching for future top management prospects we will find them among those who move from position to position occasionally to fit their own personal needs and goals. The social aspect of work is secondary to this type of person.

Promoting from within sounds great, but maybe the best people are brought in from other organizations. This trend can be seen today when we observe top people moving from General Motors or Chrysler to Ford or American Motors.

In responses to question 38, 65% of the managers state that *indecisiveness* in subordinates is their major fault. If only subordinates would speak up and give their true opinions, many benefits would accrue to all concerned. They don't want to "rock the boat," so they are afraid to be themselves.

Initiative seems indigenous to top management personnel but not to those who fail to reach higher positions. Fear of failure hobbles even the most brilliant mind and the only way to be sure one never fails is to never do anything that entails risk. As most managers know, the measured risk is the "name of the game." One should look for the sensible risk taker as a potential manager.

Most executives, according to responses to question 39, are not looking for their own replacement. Management principles state that you should always have an eye out for your own replacement to give you mobility if an even better opportunity presents itself. Of those who are looking for a replacement, 80% say one is not easy to find.

In reply to question 40, 63% said less than 10% of any group are the doers. This fits well with the old slogan that in any organization 10% of the people do 90% of the work. The executives who answered this questionnaire seem to know their people well.

Most executives are looking forward to retirement (question 41). This response seems odd when one considers the highly motivated, hard-driving type of person who is under study.

Question 42 responses reveal that 88% of executives surveyed believe most people prefer to be led rather than to make their own decisions. This concurs with earlier findings about initiative. Initiative does not appear to be common except in the higher management ranks. Leaders had the initiative before they became executives, and it helped get them the promotions.

Responses to question 43 show that 67% of the executives tend to worry a lot about work. This is natural, because it's probably what makes them good executives.

An overwhelming 83% of the executives put work over home interests (question 44). This is good for business, but bad for the home and family life. It is one of the prices they pay and they know it. And 58% say they don't spend enough time on outside activity.

The executives are about evenly split on whether or not they would do it all the same way again (question 46). Psychologists say that all things being the same, we would tend to repeat.

In selecting from a list of mistakes managers made in their careers (question 47), 33% said they were too timid at first (Sloan of General Motors said this about himself). Also, 29% said they didn't enjoy other interests enough. This is the price they paid to get where they are. Perhaps if they spent enough time on other activities they wouldn't have attained the high position they enjoy today.

Most managers (96%) say they learned a great deal from others after leaving school.

In discussing their eventual replacement, most executives (92%) say the new person should run the show his or her own way, not as the old manager ran it. This is consistent with the character of these executives. They want to run things their way and, logically, they say the new executive should run things his or her own way.

Of the questionnaires returned, 71% came from representatives of large businesses and 29% from executives operating small companies.

It is of interest to note that some common characteristics exist for the executive type of person. Even though he is generally envied for the success he has achieved, like anyone else, he bought and paid for it in other ways.

In comparison to the average person, the top manager hears a different drummer and marches to a different beat. Each individual must decide whether this beat is better or worse than any other.

I have met few people who have not got out of life everything they really wanted if they were willing to pay the price. Some complain that they never had a chance. I believe everyone gets a chance, as luck is random. It's what we do about it when it comes that matters. Do we recognize an opportunity? I believe most do, but many are deterred by inertia or fear of failure.

What separates the men from the boys or the women from the girls is willingness to take the risk to seize the opportunity. There is no high reward without high risk or payment of some kind. If you do not choose to accept the risk or make the payment, then success may elude you. It appears that the men and women discussed in this study seized opportunity as it came, paid the price, and reached some desired goal. They knew what they wanted, they planned for it, and they achieved it.

These people create, develop, expand, and leave behind something that survives them. They are a group of doers who have done a great deal of good for themselves and for many others.

1
Attitude Problems

He is quite a three-pipe problem.
—*Sir Arthur Conan Doyle*

Your attitude is what makes you uniquely you. And attitude plays the most important role in your career advancement.

As we mature on the job, we all learn much in our relationships with the people with whom we work, in mastering difficult problems, and in sometimes seeing our ideas put to work. The attitude with which we approach all our tasks eventually shapes our individual style and determines our career success or failure.

A cooperative person can do just about any job. Most jobs don't require a genius mentality or creative talent. Whatever your job, the work is a mix of repetitive routine, challenging problems, and sometimes exciting breakthroughs, but the work doesn't overwhelm you continually.

Failure on the job that often leads to disciplinary action, arguments, transfers, dismissals, or legal action is caused by attitude problems.

Some years ago, while working for the government in Washington, I attended a series of lectures for first-line managers and supervisors. The lecturer, an expert in the field of personnel management, told us two things that I have never forgotten because later experience proved him to be correct on both counts.

The first was this statement: "Show me any organiza-

15

tion's sick leave records, and I will show you payday." Sick leave is low on paydays and up the day following. This has proved to be true wherever I have worked, and other managers also confirm this observation.

Government personnel records, according to the lecturer, showed that when people had difficulties at work resulting in demotions, dismissals, involuntary transfers, or forced retirements, the reason in 89% of the cases was personality or attitude problems. My experience and that of others with whom I have talked concur with this estimate.

On page one of the July 20, 1978, issue of *The Wall Street Journal* was a brief article on job dissatisfaction. The article said that the results of a survey conducted by a private business research group indicated 87% of the workers surveyed were very satisfied or satisfied with their jobs. About 10% were dissatisfied, and 3% very dissatisfied.

Note the 13% potential problem employee group. Attitude problems usually come from a small minority at work, but those few can wreak havoc if left unattended. When, for any reason, a person refuses to cooperate with or accept the authority of another person, or is dissatisfied most of the time, the problem is unsolvable in approximately 90% of the cases.

Early in my career I tried to help a young secretary who carried her problems to work. When I heard her crying over her typewriter, I rushed over to try to help. She poured out her troubles to me at length about boyfriends, her family, her car, her job. She found little time for work. When I finally had enough and tried to get her to do some work, she resisted and did not talk to anyone for days.

I am not a guidance counselor, but I know you can't get any work done when your secretary won't even speak to you. After struggling with this situation on and off for the better part of a year, I finally gave up. I failed to help or change her attitude. I asked her to leave. Her replacement was a gem who worked with me for over seven years with never a cross word or problem. She had a good attitude about work. It was a pleasure to see her smiling face each morning.

I had made a mistake that is common in younger managers or junior supervisory personnel. I tried to help someone with an attitude problem, and I failed. You should know that if you try, the odds are better than 9 to 1 against your succeeding. The experience of many others tells the same story.

The reasons for a person having an attitude problem are so deep-rooted and complex that you won't ever solve it. If you are not a psychiatrist, you are not even qualified to try. Generally, we make it worse because we really don't know what we are doing.

In the years since, on occasion, I have tried to work with other attitude problems. My failure rate is 100%. Other managers advise me that they had no success either in trying to cope with the attitude problem.

If, for any reason, you find you are having some sort of continuing problem with a superior or a subordinate, I can suggest only one solution with any confidence.

First, try for an open discussion of the problem and try to find a solution so you can at least work together on the job. If you find that you are unable to discuss it, or if the problem recurs, then the best solution is to break off the relationship, and the sooner the better for both parties.

When you talk to someone with whom you are having problems, be careful how you conduct yourself. If you make a comment such as, "I notice you seem disturbed most of the time; what's wrong?" you may wish you had never asked. That person may pour out his soul to you. Unable to really solve deep-seated personal problems, you can very quickly get in over your head. Don't try to help alone. Get assistance from higher-ups before you try.

Also, in response to a tale of woe, avoid the reply, "I

understand." That simple remark is often misinterpreted by the troubled employee to mean, "I approve." The employee may later tell you and others, in all honesty, that you approved. Your senior manager will then ask you why you let this problem go on when you knew about it and even approved of it.

If the problem is with your boss, then you had better leave before the situation grows worse. You can't fight city hall, so leave before the explosion, which will come sooner or later if an attitude problem or personality conflict exists.

If the problem is with a subordinate, you don't have to leave, but you have to make the employee leave. Although this is difficult, it is better to face up to it sooner than later. Forcing someone out after a big blowup can hurt your career.

If you go through several similar situations over a period of years, top management probably will conclude that you must be more than 50% of the problem. Management may not ever openly discuss it with you but may find someone other than you for the next promotion.

The attitude problem is an incurable virus for which we should know some of the symptoms. This will enable us to be aware of its presence as early as possible. If you must attempt to solve it, remember past experience shows you have only about a 10% chance of any hope of success.

A person may develop an attitude problem after a transfer to a new job or a new supervisor. Such a problem is caused, in part, internally and may be just a clash of two personalities. A reassignment may solve it (unless it recurs in the next job or with the next boss as well). With persons recently promoted to a higher position, the reason could be the new job.

A personal tragedy (death, sickness, accident, or divorce) could result in the sudden change in a person's attitude at work. Most such problems are temporary while the person adjusts to the new situation. In such cases, we owe the person our compassion and assistance. However, if three or four months go by without a return to normal, there may be a permanent change in attitude or personality. This may become a serious problem that requires referral to a qualified professional if the person is willing to seek and follow professional guidance. Unfortuantely, in some such situations, persons refuse to admit to any problem.

Whatever the cause, people reveal attitude problems in the following ways:

1. They require extra time, attention, and direction. When left on their own, these persons tend to go wrong over and over again, and they always can explain their problems if given a chance. Problems seem to them to be caused by others.

2. They arrive late to work and depart early. When questioned about this, they say what's important is not how long one is at work, but what one does while there. Also, many say they are professionals and don't operate by the clock. Yet, they rarely stay late to finish a job. They never seem to give a full day's work. Their interests are clearly elsewhere.

3. They ignore legitimate authority or directions from their bosses because "they know the job better" than the boss or anyone else. They are not ever to be questioned and they resent it bitterly when they are.

4. They have difficulty in communicating with others. They prefer to be left alone. They neither ask help nor give it.

5. They exhibit strange or unusual behavior at work.

6. These people read and study all company rules and regulations and become "barracks or sea lawyers." Whenever anyone in the organization has any problem, this type usually can quote and interpret the policies and procedures, chapter and verse.

7. Such persons constantly criticize and ridicule the

boss, co-workers, the job, the building, the weather. They are never satisfied. Something is always wrong.

8. They rarely smile or tell a joke. Life is far too serious and mixed up for such levity.

9. They enjoy seeing others make mistakes, especially superiors. Instead of offering assistance, these people turn and walk away, or, worse, publicize the mistake to make sure everyone knows about it.

10. They need and request all sorts of special consideration, such as advanced leave, early departure from work, pay advances, special assignments, special working hours, special working conditions and equipment.

11. They use up all sick leave as soon as accrued, at regular, predictable intervals.

12. This type has so many troubles outside of work with their spouse, children, relatives, and neighbors, that they find it difficult to do the job. They always are ready to tell their troubles to any listener.

Since experience shows that you have less than a 10% chance of ever making a productive employee out of any with these attitude problems, the return on investment is far too low for you to spend much time trying to straighten them out. You want to spend your time and effort on those who deserve your attention, and who, in response, will do the most for themselves and for you, too. Separate yourself from attitude and behavior problems as soon as you can identify them. Don't let your conscience trouble you because these people probably got that way a long time ago before you ever met them and will never change.

There is some preventive action you can take to keep as many problem employees as possible out of your organization. The fewer you admit, the fewer you have to deal with later on. Be thorough in screening candidates before you hire them. Set the standards you require and don't lower them, regardless of the pressure if you have to expand rapidly and the top brass tells you to staff up in a hurry.

Before and during the interview, check the following items to weed out candidates with possible attitude or behavior problems:

1. Check to see if the applicant has changed jobs many times (say every year or two). He or she may be what is called a "grasshopper" who jumps around a lot or is put out. I have seen applicants with seven or eight jobs in less than a 10-year period.

2. Look to see a person's reason for leaving a former job, and ask why he or she wants to join your organization.

3. Ask if you can check several references, not personal, but with former supervisors. If an applicant doesn't want you to, then look out. Has he or she had trouble with former supervisors or employers?

4. Does the applicant criticize former bosses or places of employment? If so, listen carefully.

5. Is the applicant neat? Did he or she come to the interview on time? Does the interviewee act superior?

6. Are there any time gaps in the applicant's résumé? If so, ask why.

7. If a person asks for any special consideration or rules waiver, be careful. This is not a good sign. This doesn't refer to special consideration for physical disability, which is valid and should be considered. It means advanced vacation, advanced pay, requests for different working hours, time off during the day for personal problems, or refusal to stay late.

8. Do applicants want you to wait for them to arrive at their convenience, or will they accept an arrival time of convenience to you?

9. Ask applicants what their career goals are, and listen carefully. Many times you may not like what you hear in reply.

10. Ask applicants if they have any special personal problems or situations that could possibly affect their work.

11. Ask applicants if they have ever been convicted of any crime. You may still want to hire the person. This is not to say that you shouldn't give someone a second chance. But you have a right to know if you think such a history might affect work, other employees, clients, or the company. At the present time, I believe you can ask if the applicant has ever been convicted of a crime, but you can't ask if a person has been arrested.

12. Ask an applicant a question about anything that requires a long answer or formulation of an opinion to be explained to you. Sit back for 10 or 15 minutes, say as little as you can, and listen. Then form your opinion: Do you want him or her or not?

13. Have someone else interview the applicant and then talk to him or her and compare notes. If you agree, you know what to do. If not, then you make a decision one way or the other, and later on you will know.

No matter how carefully you screen and interview applicants, some who have attitude problems will get through. Some persons learn how to get by the interview and let it all out later. But careful interviewing can help you detect some, and it is worthwhile to avoid hiring potential problem employees.

2
Committees and Meetings

People can be motivated to be good not by telling them
that hell is a place where they will burn, but by telling
them it is an unending committee meeting. On judgment
day, the Lord will divide people by telling those on His
right hand to enter His Kingdom and those on His left to
break into small groups.
—*The Reverend Robert Kennedy,
as quoted in the* Boston Globe *(March 6, 1978)*

The dictionary definition of a committee is "a group of
people officially delegated to perform a function, as inves-
tigating, considering, reporting, or acting on a matter."

Those of us who have been selected to serve on various
committees can testify about endless meetings to discuss
trivia, listen to bad jokes, and drink cold coffee from paper
cups, while seated on metal undertaker chairs.

Perhaps if committees were better organized, most of
them could serve a more useful function. Well-run committees can accomplish tasks that are beyond the scope of
any one person. Committee members who are experts in a
variety of fields may gather, review, and report on special
aspects of an issue under study. The members should listen carefully to the other members to learn what else is
involved other than one's own special area of interest. In
this way one can benefit from committee activity. It rarely
happens this way, of course, because most of us are too
busy talking to do any listening.

As for acting on any subject, I tend to disagree with the dictionary definition of the functions of a committee. My own experience has taught me that committees are very slow when it's time to decide on anything. They ponder, they discuss too long, and, if not carefully controlled, they are likely to form subcommittees. These, in turn, do the same again and, like some evil malignancy, re-form in an almost endless repetitive process until they develop a life of their own.

Since committees are going to be with us for all of our working lives and beyond, it might be useful to set up some procedures to make the committee a more effective tool to accomplish our goals. Let us list some techniques to use within the committee to make the best use of the time spent at meetings.

Here are some rules to use when setting up a committee:

1. Define, in writing, exactly why you want to form a committee. What will be its purpose? How will it function? Be explicit, not vague. Avoid generalities. If the reason for forming the committee is vague, then the committee's findings will likely be vague. It's difficult to be precise when we are not too sure of what we are doing or why.

2. Select some *one* person as chairperson to be responsible for the success or failure of the committee. So advise this person, in advance and in writing, and receive back, in writing, an acceptance of this responsibility.

3. Agree in advance (with the chairperson's approval) on a date by which the committee must write the final report and disband. Permanent committees should be rare below the very highest level in your company or organization. Most committees should have a built-in self-destruct mechanism. Permanent committees become less effective as time goes on. They become social gatherings or places to go when one has nothing better to do. Laughter and chatter accompany these meetings, but little real work ever

gets done. I have to admit to the ladies that what they always suspected is true. Men gossip far more than women do at work.

4. Let the chairperson choose the members and assign the tasks. When all are responsible, then no one is.

5. Do not form subcommittees.

6. Avoid meetings over lunch or dinner. If the food is good, it is too enjoyable to think serious thoughts. If the food is bad, then everyone is in a bad mood and will argue rather than discuss the points at issue. Work first and eat later. A committee meeting is not a social affair.

7. Assign each committee member a role and don't allow departure from it at the meetings when the member reports on his or her phase of the issue. During discussions, of course, a free exchange is encouraged.

8. Limit the length of each meeting. Most work should be done outside the meeting and then reported on at the meeting. Give each member an allotted time to speak. Talkative members will quickly learn how to use their time effectively if they are cut off once in a while in midsentence.

An unfortunate quirk in human nature compels us to talk or write at length when we know little or nothing about the subject at hand. The less we know, the longer we talk. If you know the answer, you write or state it succinctly. If you don't know the answer, you present a ponderous essay that skirts the issue. Few people seem to have the honesty and courage to say simply, "I don't know."

9. If members are not doing their jobs, replace them. A committee is not a training ground. It is not fair to waste the time of other members.

10. The chairperson should be constantly in charge, and everyone should know this at all times. If he or she can't attend a scheduled meeting, then cancel it. The leader should always be present.

Enough of strategy. Let us now consider procedures as to how to utilize the committee at the meetings.

1. Keep meetings as formal as possible. Send out announcements far enough in advance so each member has time to prepare.

2. Tell each person who is to attend what is expected from him or her.

3. Have an agenda and stick to it. Don't have meetings to "kick around" an idea because nothing will be settled.

4. Have comfortable, well-ventilated, but not lavish surroundings. If the meetings are kept to one or two hours, members don't need coffee to keep awake.

5. If you invite outside members to attend, tell them what you expect them to do. If they come to listen, tell them in advance you will want a written report on what they got out of it. No one is neutral; each attendant either helps with the solution or adds to the problem.

6. Keep the size of the committee as small as possible. The more members, the longer the meetings become and the less people listen or actively participate. In my opinion, three is best and five or six is the maximum size of a committee that will be effective.

7. Keep small talk or side conversations to a minimum. Nothing is more distracting than a meeting in which several groups talk among themselves.

8. Encourage controversy, not agreement, but keep it polite. A participant might say, "I have information which, in my opinion, leads me to a different conclusion." Comments should not be personal. The committee must work together to be effective.

9. Always summarize at the end of each committee meeting. Tell what was accomplished, what was not, and, if possible, why. Give action items to each member to be completed and reported at the next meeting.

10. When polling the committee, let everyone have his or her say with no interruptions. If members are afraid to

disagree with the chairperson or someone else in attendance, they become almost useless.

11. Try to have members of equal rank on the committee. People will be less open or likely to disagree if superiors are also committee members.

12. Start the meeting on time and end it on time. It's best to announce before you start when it will end.

13. Have the minutes of the meeting typed and issued within one day after each meeting ends. This shows that the chairperson believes the meetings and the committee members' time are important.

14. The final report or decision has to be written to satisfy the chairperson. In fairness, though, the chairperson should include minority or dissenting opinions if there are any. Some chairpersons fear that later events may prove a minority opinion to be the correct one.

If you try to follow some of the procedures given here, you can improve upon your performance and help make a committee truly effective.

3
The Communication Problem

Evil communications corrupt good manners.
—Paul's Epistle to the Romans

We live today in a world of euphemisms. As long as we use nice words, we can mention any subject. On television we hear about "wetness problems." No one perspires or sweats any more. One hears the statement "Tell it like it is," but the people who do so are sure to be disliked by the majority of those with whom they work. Few of us are able to tolerate unvarnished truth delivered in direct language. We reject the message and despise the messenger if we don't like what is being said.

Most of us search for the "right" words to express what we feel in the least offensive manner. This is fine unless we concern ourselves more with the format of the message than its substance. Euphemisms carry us far from the truth into the world of unreality or outright lies.

When one reads that some high-level diplomats had a "meaningful meeting with a vigorous exchange of ideas and concepts," this means they didn't agree on anything.

One sometimes reads that a company has introduced a new, fully automated production facility, thereby freeing production workers from dull, repetitive tasks to do more creative, self-fulfilling work. It really means the company automated the production line to save money and laid off many production workers.

Trash collectors are now sanitary engineers, and ditchdiggers are land relocation experts. During the recent recession, a number of formerly employed managers and technical personnel suddenly became "consultants." For whom they consult and how much they earn seems not to matter. In truth, many consult for no one.

Even the term *communication problem* or *gap* has become a euphemistic catchall. In an interview a famous television news analyst said he and his twenty-one-year-old daughter had some differences that she called a communication problem. As a television reporter who knew something about communicating, he said communication was not the problem.

The daughter communicated to him what she wanted to do. The father clearly communicated to her his disapproval and rejection of her plans. They both understood each other very well. They didn't have a communication problem. They had a disagreement.

If you ever want to hear the plain truth of what the other person really thinks about a situation, one way to get it is to make the other person angry. When someone is angry with you, he forgets about your feelings or using nice words. He will tell you in a clear and loud voice exactly what he thinks about you and the situation that exists between him and you. He may even go back a bit in time and bring up long forgotten or suppressed problems. It may not be good for your ego and it may hurt a little, but you will know what he thinks.

In business and elsewhere, there are three basic types of communication: upward, downward, and sideward (within or between peer groups). The communication process varies, depending upon which of the three types of communication one is doing. We deliver the same message in three different ways, depending upon the situation at the time.

Problems in communication arise when the person doing the communicating is unaware of or doesn't care which of the three types he or she is doing (upward, sideward, or downward).

A foreman can communicate his dissatisfaction with the performance of the production crew in clear, concise language. He would be wise to pass the same information upward to the general manager in more formal, less explicit terms, but the same message should get through to both recipients.

It is axiomatic that the messages upward are often less truthful than the other two types. This is why upper management tries to maintain several separate lines of communication down into the organization. It is not that they think people deliberately lie. It's just that they understand human nature.

Those of you below the higher echelon in your organizations should not resent it if you see this going on. When you get to those higher positions, you too will, in all likelihood, do the same crosschecking of your sources of information to find out exactly what is going on within the organization.

Communication downward tends to be authoritative and quick. Directives or orders are issued to be carried out. Little or no explanation is given as to the reasons behind the directives. "Dad, can I have $10 and the car tonight?" Answer: "No." That's quick, clear communication. The young person now tells his or her friends that there is a communication problem with Dad. The problem isn't in communication at all. Dad knows what he was requested to do. He didn't want to do it and clearly said so.

Open feedback or comment on these directives is generally discouraged in practice, if not in principle. Let the subordinate who points out that the boss was wrong beware. The job he loses may be his own.

For the customer who pays the bill, the "customer is

always right" still stands as one of the few unchanging verities by which business operates. Never argue with customers or prove them wrong. You will become the most honest person in the unemployment line.

Communication between peers (or sideward) tends to be by mutual consent. Since no one has any real authority over others in the peer group, one has to use logic and persuasion to elicit agreement and get any action. This sort of communication can become quite difficult.

Upward communication is by far the most difficult and trying on the subordinate. How does one communicate with a superior if one wants to differ or correct an error that came from above? No one I have ever met enjoys being corrected or shown to be in error. Do it carefully.

Several years ago, I carefully selected from a catalog what I thought was a pleasing and comfortable set of office furniture. When it arrived and was all set up, I called in my secretary and asked her how (not if) she liked it. She said she didn't like it much and she pointed out my errors in judgment in mismatching colors and chairs and in the arrangement of the furniture. She was, or course, quite correct. I know nothing about interior decorating.

I had to force myself to admire her honesty. Eventually I realized that she was really upset because I had not consulted her in advance, which I should have done. She wanted to help and I didn't let her. She did not tell me the real reason she was upset. I had to figure that out for myself.

The upward type of communication calls for tact, because the subordinate may have to contradict or correct the superior in a manner that does not anger him, downgrade his position, or damage his ego. For example, don't ever say to a boss, "You're wrong." Bosses don't like that kind of communicating.

The subordinate, in effect, must elicit a reaction or behavior in the superior much as a salesman makes someone want to buy a product.

In the extreme, the subordinate who continually delivers unpleasant or unwelcome news to his or her superior runs a great risk of no promotion, no raise, or involuntary transfer or dismissal. Don't count on your boss being such a well-adjusted person that he or she is above the ego-shattering experience of learning that some subordinates know more about the job than the boss does. This disturbs some managers. Some are pleased about it. Some view it as a threat. The best advice is to know well the manager with whom you communicate, and act accordingly.

When all communication stops for whatever reason, that is not a communication problem. The problem lies elsewhere, not in communication.

So what do we really mean when we use the term *communication problem?* First, we must admit that the problem, whatever it is, is generally not in communicating. The problem lies somewhere else. In order to cure any illness or solve any problem, it is best to find the ultimate cause. There are proximate causes, ultimate causes, and others in between in the chain of cause and effect.

The proximate cause of a patient's discomfort may be a rash that makes the patient uncomfortable. A doctor can give the patient some salve that stops the itch and possibly clears up the rash temporarily. In this case, the doctor cures the proximate cause of the patient's discomfort. This, however, is the effect of another cause which is whatever is creating the rash in the first place. If the doctor proceeds to additional tests and discovers the patient has an allergy of some sort and solves that problem, he or she solves the underlying and ultimate cause of the problem. There is no longer a rash to treat because the ultimate cause has been located and eliminated.

When we spend our time and effort in trying to solve

communication problems, in most cases we are applying salve to the rash. It is only temporary and will recur because we are seeing a manifestation of something that is the effect of some other more basic cause.

It is difficult enough to solve problems even when we know the real cause. It is almost impossible to solve them when we either don't know the real cause, address our efforts in the wrong direction, or treat the effect of some other remote problem.

Did you ever observe people trying to communicate with someone who doesn't speak their language? They repeat themselves and raise their voices, "reasoning" that the other person will suddenly become fluent in the English language. When we find we can't communicate, we become angry and blame others because they don't speak our language.

This is an example of trying to solve the wrong problem. The person being spoken to isn't deaf; he just doesn't understand English. This isn't a communication problem; it's a language barrier. The solution is to find someone who speaks both languages to interpret for you. Then you can communicate even by whispering.

If we try to locate and isolate the ultimate cause rather than the proximate cause of a problem, at least we are working in the right direction. Even if we are unable to solve the problem, we have identified it and can assist by referring a person to a qualified professional.

4
Criticism

People ask you for criticism, but they only want praise.
—*Somerset Maugham,* Of Human Bondage,

Criticism is the act of making judgments, or passing an unfavorable judgment, censuring, or disapproving. It is human nature that most judgment or criticism is more negative than positive. An unfavorable judgment is what most people mean when they use the word *criticism.*

Criticism is something most people would rather give than receive. It can be helpful when properly applied and properly received, but criticism is usually poorly given and poorly received. We must constantly remind ourselves that criticism, like medicine, tastes bad, but may be good for us, so we swallow hard and take it, but most of us don't like it.

The emotional response from many people when they are subjected to criticism is sometimes so great and immediate that little or no benefit accrues. Most people know this, so they suffer through many painful situations, because they don't know how or are afraid to criticize anyone about anything.

Traditionally, there are two ways to get the truth from someone: get him or her either drunk or angry. In neither state do people consider your feelings. They just want to say what they have always held back, and alcohol or anger loosens these inhibitions.

Criticism is necessary in many business situations. There are opposing schools of thought about how to conduct the critical interview. One view is to start and end the interview with some compliments to ease the pain of the blow which you must deliver. Another group says not to mix praise with criticism, because the person on the receiving end may remember only the good words and forget the criticism. Either method has to be used with tact.

It is just about impossible to write a how-to list for criticism. There are too many variables in time, circumstances, and people. However, you may find helpful the following how-not-to list when criticizing anyone.

1. *Don't get personal.* When people are in the mood to criticize, they tend to get personal. This hurts, creates resentment, interrupts friendly relationships, and can destroy office efficiency. If you disagree with some idea or suggestion it is better to say, "I tend to disagree with that idea or suggestion because . . ." and then give your reasons. There is no reason to attack, insult, or put down someone just because you disagree with his or her ideas or suggestions. Violent personal assaults and ridicule are the most effective ways to stop all ideas and suggestions. People who witness the attack are as offended or frightened as the victim and will rarely, if ever again, risk putting themselves in such a situation.

Superiors sometimes use this approach on subordinates, because the subordinate is almost defenseless from such as assault. He or she can't really strike back. Some people do it as a matter of course with anything or anyone they criticize.

Authors of books and articles published in various popular magazines or business and technical journals are subject to this type of personal criticism. Letters to the editor in a later edition many times contain some personal remark about the author of an article or book, followed by a criticism of whatever the author has written.

Since most critics do not know the author, personal derision is uncalled for and inappropriate. An author expects disagreement about what he or she writes and most welcome it because it stimulates new ideas and approaches. But personal criticism from someone who doesn't even know you is a bit hard to take, much more so than from some co-worker or boss whom you know, work with, and respect.

Just after Pearl Harbor, Great Britain declared war on Japan. Winston Churchill prepared the document and summoned his representative to deliver it to the Japanese Embassy. The representative read the document and asked why Mr. Churchill was so courteous in declaring war. The prime minister replied, "When you are going to kill someone, it can't hurt to be polite."

2. *Don't discuss topics other than the one at hand.* Some people go back in time and rehash old problems to everyone's discomfort. Of course, if this is the second or third time the person has left the office door open at night, then past mistakes have to be discussed, because they relate to the same recurring mistake. But if the topic of criticism is the unlocked office door, then don't go into previous incidents in which the same person hung up the telephone on your best client or hit your new car in the parking lot.

Those problems are not germane to the case under discussion. Keep on the one subject only. It is difficult, at best, to get a positive response from the person under criticism. By adding old coals to the fire, you only generate more heat, but little light.

3. *Don't delay.* If you believe criticism is called for, do it as soon as possible, but not on the spot or in public. You may let it go entirely if several days pass before you talk to the person concerned. It is easy to delude ourselves into thinking that we didn't have time to take the corrective action.

Another reason for avoiding delay is that the person on the receiving end may well know a dressing down is in order and is waiting for it to come. If nothing happens, the person worries about it for several days and then decides the boss is either too timid or too occupied to deal with the mistake. The result is a strong possibility of a repeat performance. When you finally conduct a critical interview after several recurrences of the same event, you will surely hear such a defense as, "You didn't say anything to me about this before. Why are you singling me out for this now?" He or she has a valid point here, if you delay the criticism.

Still another reason to avoid delay is that others may be aware of the incident that deserves criticism, and if none follows, they will remember it and use it as an excuse if and when they ever are subject to criticism from the boss for any reason.

4. *Don't be negative.* If you do not know how to correct the problem or what to suggest as an improvement after you criticize someone, then it's best not to criticize in the first place. Too many of us make comments such as, "You made a mistake," or "That won't work," or "I don't like it." However, when these critics are asked what they would do instead, they fall silent. This type of negative comment does nothing but create resentment and helps no one.

Unless and until you have something to say which, in your opinion, will help a person improve performance or prevent a recurrence of a mistake, then stay silent.

5. *Don't be one way.* Don't just criticize but never compliment. Managers often say little unless they want to complain or criticize someone. Managers should be just as free with compliments as with criticism. It is a good idea to look for something good to say to and about someone who has recently been criticized. This helps restore good relations that may have become strained as a result of the criticism. It's good for the ego of the persons criticized, and they will appreciate it even if they don't show it immediately.

6. *Don't go beyond giving a second chance.* Managers

should be selective in the things they choose to criticize. Criticism should be confined to serious matters, mistakes subject to recurrence if not corrected, and situations in which you have a good chance of winning your point. If all three of these are not present, you may well be wasting your time.

Commenting upon every little fault one finds in others is useless. You should be careful in what you choose to criticize. When you do, however, the criticism should result in some improvement or action.

It is pointless to keep going back to someone about the same problem. The Navy has an old saying: "Every dog gets two bites." If an officer makes a serious mistake, he is given one more chance. If he makes the same or a similar mistake one more time, he is replaced. Some persons are repeaters, and all the comments or criticism in the world won't change them. They refuse to learn or they are unable to change.

We all deserve a second chance, but if we repeat, we don't learn from our mistakes. Such people can be dangerous and disruptive in any organization. It also can become a waste of time and energy to try repeatedly to correct the same problem.

7. *Don't be afraid to show concern or controlled anger.* We have been schooled and trained to never show when we are upset or angry. Such displays are considered "bad form." That's one of the reasons that some managers or supervisors get heart attacks.

It is good sometimes to show concern or even some controlled anger in some situations. Some people don't think the situation is serious when a manager "keeps his cool" during the critical interview. They don't respond unless they think it is serious for them.

Letting your concern show and displaying controlled anger can have dramatic impact on the person under criticism. The anger, however, should be directed at the deed, not the person. Love the sinner; hate the sin. In demonstrating concern to the point of visible upset, the manager gets his or her point across. Immediate improvement should result. If not, further corrective action is necessary.

Of course, this technique should be used with discretion. A screamer who shouts or loses his temper frequently will never be an effective leader. Sometimes, in certain situations, with some people, a display of controlled anger can be more effective than a polite interview. You have to know with whom you are dealing at the time, and react accordingly. Such a show of concern or display of controlled anger should be limited to situations that can be corrected or improved by such tactics. Some people react only to a visible demonstration.

If, in your opinion, the problem merits serious corrective action up to and including dismissal, then anger or emotional outbursts are never in order. Never punish anyone when you are angry. When you have to dismiss someone, do it politely.

You owe such a person a calm and reasonable statement as to why he or she is going to be disciplined or dismissed. After the shock wears off, such persons may remember what was said, and it will help them in their next assignment or new position. As a manager, you have an obligation to, at least, give it a try.

5
Disagreements

There is no man so friendless but what he can find a friend
sincere enough to tell him disagreeable truths.
—*Edward George Earle Lytton*

Disagreement, if handled properly, yields positive
benefits. Association with only those who do things your
way or always agree with you may be comfortable, but it is
not always productive.

A wise manager encourages those with other points of
view to express their ideas. Those who sometimes disagree
may well have something of value to contribute if their
viewpoints are not shut off. It is up to those in charge to
create an environment that neither suppresses disagreement nor permits disagreement to degenerate into
hostility and distrust. A manager who skillfully handles
disagreement will not permit employees to "talk the thing
to death" without ever reaching constructive conclusions.

Handling disagreements requires the exercise of good
judgment and some knowledge of personality traits. Let us
consider some of the types of personalities in the workplace:

1. *The know-it-all.* This person tells everyone what he
thinks—loud and clear. He is rarely there when a decision
has to be made, but is right there afterward telling you and
everyone else why he disagreed with what was done. He
uses 20/20 hindsight to tell you what was wrong. He is
never wrong.

2. *The shy person.* These personalities are so quiet you scarcely know they are around. They do their work as assigned to them. They rarely venture an opinion or disagree with anyone. They don't want to hurt anyone's feelings, so if they believe something is going to go wrong, they don't say anything. They would never presume to suggest to the boss or anyone else that there is a better way to do anything. That could cause controversy, and this type doesn't like to be the subject of controversy or in any way involved.

3. *The "I only follow orders type."* These people do what they are told and don't ask questions. They may disagree or give their ideas when asked, but unless and until they are specifically requested to give opinions, they tend to remain silent and never question anything.

4. *The born arguer.* This type likes to oppose for the sake of opposing. No matter what you plan to do or what decision you want to make, you can count on them to disagree. They seem to feel that the only way they can show you they have minds of their own is to disagree with just about everything and everyone. This is usually a form of arrested emotional development.

5. *The reasonable type.* These personalities are willing and able to contribute ideas and are not afraid to disagree or to offer novel ideas, if they are given the right environment in which to respond. Fortunately, the majority of employees are in this category.

Management should develop a climate for those in category 5 to be able to express disagreement or propose new and better ways to do things. On occasion, even those in categories 1, 2, 3, and 4 offer some good ideas. Remember, even a broken clock is correct twice a day. People in categories 1–4 are few enough to be handled on an individual basis. Set up the system to take care of the majority, and take the others as they come one at a time. But don't let the disruptive few upset your system to encourage and receive comments or disagreement from the majority.

Let's assume you are the manager responsible for a group of people. You have to assign work to other people and monitor the progress through one or several layers of intermediate managers. You have to make decisions, many times based upon information others bring to you. You are responsible for the organization's efforts, and you want people to come to you with their ideas, and to disagree if they think what is going to be done is wrong or could be done better. You can't have the entire organization second-guessing everything you do. You know they all don't agree with everything you do. You don't want silence and blind agreement with all of your decisions either.

Somewhere in between those two extremes is what you want. Exactly where it lies, and how you get there, depends upon your personality and judgment, the environment in which you work, and to what extent you set up procedures and conduct yourself so a free interchange of ideas and disagreement can be maintained.

Suggestion boxes are nice for morale, but generally little of lasting value comes out of them. Such suggestions as more parking spaces, better coffee in the coffee machines, or better cafeteria food are what one sees most often in these boxes.

Management should develop some techniques so those at the lower end of the chain of command may be able to disagree or try to change things and know they will be heard and their ideas given consideration. Following are some possible techniques. All of them may not apply in any one environment. It is up to you to decide where and when they fit and if they should be used.

1. *No questions asked, just do it.* There are times, unfortunately, when some new directive must be implemented and there is no choice; examples are new IRS regulations,

increases in Social Security deductions, new laws, and safety regulations. Such changes must be made, and no amount of talking or disagreement will alter that need. Modifying such rules is beyond the control of the company.

It's up to management in such cases to clearly explain what is about to happen and why. Also, it should be made clear no exceptions will be permitted. Get it over and done with as soon as possible. Added discussions accomplish nothing.

2. *The boss wants ideas now.* In this situation the manager has a decision or a plan to make, involving complex issues, most likely about some future event. The wise manager tries to gather information from past experience on the subject at hand. What happened before; why; is it likely to occur again? What, if anything, is different about current plans? The boss, about to take a business risk, asks for input from others up and down the line.

Now you may freely discuss the topic at hand. You may agree or disagree as you like, but the boss has the right to accept or reject your ideas. A manager considers other opinions from people whose judgment he respects, but he has to make the ultimate decision. In choosing the final course of action, the boss should explain why the decision was made and why some other suggestions were eliminated.

Unless the decision maker does this, he will find, after a while, that those whose ideas were not accepted will fall silent, because they believe they are not given any serious attention. Critics may not be creative, but they have a valid role in giving new insight or noting imperfections in any plan. The trick is to get their reaction before, not after, the decision is made, in time to reexamine the plan. If you are among those asked to contribute your ideas, consider it a compliment. If you are the boss who asks for ideas and criticism of your plans, consider yourself fortunate if you receive honest, dissenting opinions before you act, because you, most surely, will get them afterward.

3. *Unsolicited advice or disagreement.* Know that if you offer unsolicited advice, you walk on dangerous ground. Few people easily accept unsolicited advice or disagreement. Before you do this, carefully consider the potential consequences. You can emerge as a hero or a bum, depending upon how the boss accepts what you say and upon whether or not later events prove you to be right or wrong. You can lose out in either case sometimes.

Before you take this step, I suggest you know the person very well, proceed carefully at each step, and be prepared to stop quickly when you meet resistance. By presuming upon a friendship or close relationship with a boss and giving unsought advice or disagreement, you put your career on the line. I don't say never do it, but be careful when you do. It doesn't work out too often. Be sure you do it before the action takes place, not afterward.

If you elect this dangerous approach, I suggest the following scenario for your consideration: Ask the boss if you may speak to him or her about the issue at hand. Carefully explain that you realize your advice or comments were not solicited. Then ask if he or she would like to hear your comments. Don't go on unless the answer is a definite yes. Don't write unsolicited memos. Say it in private. Tell no one else, especially if the boss accepts your comments and changes the decision or plan. Don't do it again. The boss will invite you, in the future, if he or she wants your advice again. Once is enough, because this type of meeting generally involves a disagreement. Few people ever go to a superior on their own to tell him or her they agree with what was planned. From silence, one assumes general agreement.

4. *After-action review.* The wise manager solicits com-

ments on a plan or decision after it has been put into effect—especially so with a successful plan. People are much more prone to give honest advice or disagreement about a plan that has worked out than about a failure. People are not afraid to speak out about the smaller things that go wrong. Since those things can be corrected in the future, that is precisely what the boss wants.

Unsolicited after-action disagreement from anyone concerning an unsuccessful plan or decision is so obviously dangerous that only the most foolhardy would ever attempt it.

In any disagreement, whenever possible, try to give your opponent an opportunity to "save face." In winning your argument, do not force the issue to a point where the other has to admit a mistake before corrective action follows.

It is only human to bitterly resist being boxed in or proved wrong. We all have egos and will react negatively to disagreement that is based upon a criticism of our own performance, decisions, or judgments. No benefit will accrue to you if you win some point of disagreement but in so doing you offend someone else. You only gain an enemy at work. Even if he or she leaves over it, others who remain watched you operate and they will remember. At work, much like anywhere else, we need all the help and all the friends we can get. So, always keep a weather eye out during a disagreement that you won't hurt any feelings or damage any egos.

In summary then, coping with disagreement and dissent can be beneficial or disruptive, depending upon how it is done and how the individuals concerned react to it. It requires special effort and maturity on both sides. It can be judged only by evaluating the long-term effects. If it works for you, use it; if not, don't.

The issues about which disagreement is discussed here

are not moral or ethical. I'm discussing pragmatic, business-type decisions. When it comes to disagreement on a moral, legal, or ethical level, you should, of course, follow your conscience and never compromise it. Some people have compromised their moral codes to their later sorrow, both public and private.

You should go directly to the person with whom you disagree on a moral issue or point of ethics, tell him or her why, and then decide whether you want to leave or whether you can stay and change what offends you.

6
The Disciplinary Interview

It will be your duty not only to set an example of discipline and perfect steadiness under fire, but also to maintain the most friendly relations with those whom you are leading. —*Lord Kitchener*

The disciplinary interview (DI) usually occurs after a major offense for which dismissal could result or after a series of minor offenses that cause concern to the boss and/or fellow workers.

In many larger companies, a DI can be quite formal, involving management personnel and perhaps union representatives for the one to be disciplined. Others who are somehow involved may be there to testify. In government and some nongovernment jobs, the DI approaches the legal or semi-legal status of a courtroom.

You should not call for a number of DI's. It is disturbing to everyone concerned and, even if you win your case, you may acquire an unfortunate reputation as someone who cannot handle his or her people or is too strict or severe in supervising others. In either situation, you are the loser. The young teacher who sends too many pupils to the principal's office for discipline will eventually be called in to explain why.

Before you reach the stage of a formal DI, I strongly recommend that you try, informally, to solve the problem by a quiet chat, some encouragement, a transfer, or reassignment. In many, but not all, situations the problem can be worked out to mutual advantage without recourse to a formal DI.

Experience indicates that most formal DI's don't solve the problem anyway. Everyone is trying to defend his or her position, and the battle lines become so drawn and fixed that there is little opportunity for give and take.

DI's are allowed to happen for any one of several reasons:

1. As part of the company's grievance procedures, the DI may be mandatory before any further action, such as dismissal, can be taken.

2. Even if you work for an organization that doesn't require a DI, some sort of formal warning should be given in all fairness to the one directly concerned.

3. The DI could reveal to higher management that the problem is the manager, and not the defendant.

4. Often, DI's are held for the morale of the other employees. People don't like to think that they can lose their jobs on someone's whim or snap judgment under stress or anger, so DI's are sometimes held even when the result is a foregone conclusion.

If there is to be a DI, then you, as the manager, had better prepare your homework in advance and take the following steps:

1. See your immediate supervisor and explain that Harry or Jane is acting up again and you think a formal DI is necessary prior to a dismissal notice if the undesirable behavior doesn't stop. At this stage, you must satisfy your boss that you have made several attempts to talk to and reason with the person. If your boss agrees that the DI is in order, proceed to the next step.

2. Find out the company's policies and procedures as to the DI and follow them to the letter. Usually, the policies require that you notify the other party some days prior to the DI to allow time to prepare a defense. A defendant

may prepare an offensive, too, against you, so consider this as a real possibility and prepare yourself.

3. Prepare your case in writing. Write every detail you can think of as the situation began to develop. (Your daily log will be invaluable in this situation. See Chapter 16.) Your case is stronger if you are able to state that other people have experienced the same or similar problems with the defendant.

4. It is important to guard against any indication that you are acting out of spite, anger, resentment, or for any personal reasons. You are acting in the best interests of the organization. You, as manager, have a problem with an individual and, with regret, you have decided it has reached the point that a formal DI must be called to settle the matter once and for all.

5. You had better show that you have tried a number of times to solve the problem informally with several warnings, but to no avail. You must show that you have clearly tried to explain the seriousness of the situation to the person concerned. You can be sure that he will deny or try to convince others that previous warnings never took place. If he can't deny them, he will try to show that he thought you weren't really serious, or you didn't make yourself clear.

A previously written memo to the person concerned, with a written response received, will stand you in good stead at the DI. Then, no one can deny your previous attempts to solve the problem informally. Keep your immediate supervisor informed during all phases of this operation. You may need his or her support at the DI.

6. You may request that other junior or senior personnel attend if they are willing and able to support your position. Don't force anyone to attend. This may win your point at the DI but create greater resentment against you later on. If your case is weak without testimony from other

willing managers and senior or junior personnel to strengthen your position, then perhaps you better think twice before you call for the formal DI.

In any DI you can safely assume that some or possibly most of the following will come up for discussion or be involved somehow:

1. The defendant may claim personal differences led to this DI. He may claim that you hate him, are jealous of him, or are afraid of him. Religious or racial prejudice may be claimed in the defense.

2. The defendant may claim that you are not a good manager and that you caused most of the problems. He will have his own facts and figures to present.

3. Upper management will bend over backward to be more than fair to the defendant, especially if union grievance procedures are involved. No one wants a strike.

4. The burden of proof lies with you, and you will probably speak first, so make it good. Your presentation should be detailed. Try to get your position fully discussed before the defendant gets his turn at bat.

5. Upper management will be represented by the director of personnel or a lawyer. A grievance committee may be present. You and your boss and the defendant and perhaps his representative will be there. Present your case quietly, forcefully, and quickly, and try to work from written material as much as possible. Verbal dueling at this stage is fruitless.

6. You will be expected to state what discipline you think is in order: suspension, fine, transfer, demotion, or dismissal. Propose only one that you have carefully thought out, and don't present alternatives. They will weaken your case. You should have thought of those before the DI.

7. Stand by to defend yourself against the counterattack.

Even if you win, it is still a bad situation. If the employee is disciplined and returns to his former position in your organization, you can expect some sort of recurrence or open resentment from him and his friends. Most formal DI's eventually result in the defendants' departures through resignations, transfers, or later dismissals. The manager may possibly resign because he believed his word or judgment was questioned during the DI.

At best, the DI is used to show all employees they have some rights that the company or organization will observe. In practice, it should be avoided at all costs. It is much like a marriage counselor trying to act as an arbitrator between a man and a woman who no longer love each other. Even if the counselor convinces the wife to remain, because she is obviously better off living in a fine house and the kids are spared the family split-up, and if the counselor convinces the husband that he is better off staying with the wife rather than going through the financial, social, and psychological trauma of a divorce, something has gone that will never return. It is a business relationship, and it should be much more than that.

If you and someone else have to go to a formal DI in order to work together, something is missing from your relationship that will never return, if it ever was there in the first place. If you as the manager require more than one DI every five years or so, it will adversely affect your career. If you are the defendant in a DI, I suggest you look for a job elsewhere, because what kind of merit increase or performance rating can you expect in the future from a boss who convenes a DI against you?

7
Dismissals

The end of a man is an action, not a thought, though it were the noblest. —Thomas Carlyle

As with everything else in life, business and work have pleasant and, at times, unpleasant aspects. One of the most disagreeable tasks is to have to dismiss anyone. It's not the same as a layoff in which a number of people are let go because of a lack of business. Firing an individual employee for cause is so unpleasant that many managers and supervisors avoid doing it, or they make mistakes when they do it.

If someone has to be terminated, it is really up to the manager or supervisor to do it. If this duty is shirked, then eventually a much worse situation develops and the manager may imperil his own career. Most managers or supervisors let problem situations go far too long before they finally act.

The person to be terminated has been given a number of warnings and disciplinary interviews or discussions about the situation. The time for termination has come. Now how do you do it? Answer: Do it coolly, calmly, and strictly by the book. Following is a list of don'ts:

1. *Never fire anyone on the spot or while you are angry.* Consider the consequences of a real-life case. A man was fired from his job on the spot, because he was caught stealing cans of paint from the factory where he worked. A security guard called the man's boss, who went out to the parking lot, took one look, and fired the employee on the spot.

The boss was so angry, he forgot the union grievance procedure. The union filed a complaint against the boss, and the man was reinstated to his job so that management could get the union grievance dropped and avoid a strike. If the boss had followed proper procedure, the union very likely would have agreed to dismiss the man.

2. *Never dismiss anyone publicly.* In anger, the one being dismissed will look for any reason to justify himself or strike back. If, in addition to being dismissed, an employee suffers the added humiliation of having it done in front of co-workers or strangers, a law suit might ensue.

3. *Never dismiss anyone on your own authority.* Whether later events prove you to be correct or not doesn't matter if, for any reason, the person is reinstated. Then you are humiliated and you will never again have any authority or influence over the reinstated employee. Perhaps even his friends at work, too, may act up a bit to teach you a lesson and challenge your authority, because to them it appears that you really don't have any where it counts.

4. *Don't be informal when dismissing anyone.* A quiet, verbal dismissal and a quick departure of the offending employee may be followed by a claim for unemployment compensation. In most states the unemployment adjustors tend to favor the applicant over his or her company. It is a little-known fact that employers pay 100% of the costs for federal and state unemployment insurance. No taxes or contributions from the employees are involved.

Since surveys indicate that 95% of all employees believe they contribute to unemployment insurance (most confuse it with Social Security deductions), they quickly file claims at the local unemployment office.

If you claim that an employee was dismissed for cause, you had better have written records to prove your claim. Since your company's contribution to unemployment insurance is computed on the basis of claims paid to your former employees, then your company has to restore to the fund any payments made to your former employees. It definitely will work to your disadvantage if you dismiss someone verbally who later gets unemployment checks. Your company president, treasurer, or controller won't like paying for it later just because you didn't keep records.

5. *Don't talk about it to any unauthorized people.* After you have dismissed someone, it is natural for people to ask you the whereabouts of the employee. If you tell them the employee was fired and the reason, your remarks may also become the basis for a law suit. If an employee can prove that your remarks in any way hurt him or hindered his chances for another job, you may have to answer in a court of law.

Going to court as the defendant is not a profitable expenditure of time and effort. Your company won't like the publicity, and this sort of thing definitely won't help your career.

6. *Never give a bad reference later.* If you cannot honestly give someone a good reference, then don't reply. Most companies understand what no reply means. If they call you and want to discuss the person, then refer them to the personnel department or your legal office. Again, the caller knows what this means.

Giving a bad reference can also result in law suits, because the next company may advise the applicant why he wasn't offered a position. This happens even though you are trying to be honest and the other company says it is all in confidence.

7. *Don't give false references either.* After the offending person leaves, things on the job improve, and passions cool down, it is natural for you to feel some regret and compassion for the former employee. We all tend to cool off with time.

Some weeks or months later, you may receive a request

for a reference. You know that the real story of the dismissal would damage the applicant. You also know that no response might hurt too, so you try to be nice and write a good, but false, reference.

Here's an example of what can happen in such situations. A person was fired for theft. It was entered in his personnel record and filed away. Later a request for a reference came in. The former boss, in trying to be a nice guy, wrote and forwarded a good recommendation to the new employer. The applicant was hired, and later escaped with a large amount of cash and valuables stolen from the new employer.

The police, in checking out the background of this person, uncovered the employment record and reason for dismissal from his former position. It was obvious that his old boss sent in a false recommendation, as it was all in the files. A law suit followed in which the person's former company was sued and had to pay damages.

All of these hazards are frightening to a junior or intermediate manager, so what should one do in handling a dismissal? Following are some recommendations that time and experience have shown to be useful:

1. Prepare a written document prior to the dismissal for your immediate supervisor, stating the reasons and your recommendations that the person be dismissed. If you can include similar written recommendations by some junior managers, so much the better.

2. Discuss the proposed dismissal with your boss in private, and get his or her concurrence in writing if possible. If the boss doesn't write it down, then you should write a confidential memo back in which you clearly state that he or she concurred with your recommendation. Keep a copy.

3. Agree with your boss on the date of dismissal.

4. On the agreed upon date, ask the employee to come

to your office after working hours, if possible. In any case, do it in private, possibly with your company lawyer or personnel manager present.

When you dismiss an employee, tell him why, pay him for a reasonable termination period, and escort him out.

5. Show no anger and don't argue. Keep it cool and businesslike.

6. If you work in a large company, you may be able to let the personnel manager handle it all. If so, turn it over and stay out of it unless company rules require your presence.

7. Tell no one about it, even at home. Members of your family may repeat it at the store, and you never know who is passing by in the aisle.

8. If people at work ask about the employee, just say he left, if you have to say anything.

As difficult as it is to dismiss employees, they generally know it is coming, and most of the worry is needless. Whenever I have had to do this most unpleasant task, employees were quiet and most said they expected it.

In dismissing someone, the manner in which it is done is just as important as the reason for which it was done. The ramifications of an improperly handled dismissal are so potentially damaging that it is advisable to find out how your company does it before you get involved in a firing.

8
Doers

Be doers of the word, not hearers only.
—Epistle of James

Doers get things done. They have initiative and they generate activity.

Three statements that pertain to doers follow:

In any organization, 90% of the work is done by 10% of the people.

There are three kinds of people in the world: 5% who do things, 10% who don't do anything but carefully study what the doers do and comment on these activities to each other, and a third group of 85% who neither do anything nor know or care what is going on.

In any sales organization, 80% to 90% of the sales are made by 20% of the sales force.

It appears then that active people who are interested in what is to be done or involved in any activity usually are in the minority, whether at work, in a church group or a bowling league, or in any activity involving more than two or three people. The same few always seem to come forward and do most of the job whatever it may be.

How does one identify a doer before one hires him or her? Do we really want an organization full of doers? Are all doers intelligent? The remainder of this chapter will discuss these questions.

If we can learn to identify, in advance, the potential doers, we can concentrate on the people from this group as future managers, salespersons, or group leaders.

You can find out if a job applicant is a doer by inquiring into one's school life. Discuss their childhood with applicants. Academic records and job résumés never tell the whole story. Did applicants organize or lead any groups in school or in the neighborhood where they lived? Are they currently active in whatever groups they belong to, such as church groups, political groups, and social organizations? If an applicant answers yes to most of these questions, you may have a doer.

This leads to the next question: Do you really want a doer for the job at hand? In most cases, I propose you may not. Since doers will become active in whatever they may be assigned to do, they look around them and see what others are doing as well. They try to help; they make suggestions; they don't accept the status quo; they question things and try to change them if they think it can be done better some new way as they see it. *They do things.*

A roomful of doers could really upset the entire organization. Everyone can't be the boss or the manager, and the boss's instructions cannot constantly be reexamined, discussed at length, and modified in infinite ways by the workforce. A group of doers will do just that. They can't help it. It is their nature. Is it then desirable to fill any organization with active doers? Perhaps it is not. When two or more doers meet, they gain strength from each other and become even more active.

Finally, to the third question: Are all doers intelligent? Unfortunately, in my opinion, they are not. Being a doer seems to be more an emotional than an intellectual quality. Those who have initiative, drive, and strength of character to do things alone and change things can wreak havoc around them if they are not too intelligent and thus change things for the worse.

An example may show my point:

Several years ago when my oldest daughter was in grammar school, I went to a PTA meeting one evening. I was discussing the plans for a fund-raising dinner with the school principal in the hall before the meeting was scheduled to start. She glanced over my shoulder toward the door, and I saw her turn white. She ran away from me into her office and closed the door. I thought she had suddenly become ill and went in to see if I could help. She pulled me into her office and asked me to remain quiet for a few minutes.

I was puzzled until she finally said that she saw Mrs. X enter the building. Mrs. X was driving the principal crazy. It seems Mrs. X was a doer with no brains. She constantly badgered the principal to do one foolish thing after another. She meant well, but soon involved everyone in one of her schemes to their ultimate sorrow. She never gave up, always had a new idea to try out, but was invariably wrong. Nothing ever worked out right. At first people felt sorry for Mrs. X, but she grated people's nerves and became unpopular.

The principal said it was very difficult as she knew Mrs. X meant well, but she couldn't stand it any more. If only someone could turn off Mrs. X. Many tried, but no one ever did. She was a doer and still is, I'm sure. Fortunately, she moved and is now "helping out" in another town far away.

Such doers may, in part, explain why almost every large organization has policies and procedures that run to many pages. These books are used by middle management in directing lower-level personnel since there is little opportunity for these managers to use initiative or judgment. If a problem comes up, they look it up in the manual. If it is in the manual, they follow the instructions step by step, as a cookbook. If the problem isn't covered by the manual, they either do nothing or write a memo to their superior about it. He or she writes another memo to the next level up. Most people accept this. It drives the doer crazy.

This system works well in large organizations. Doers will become active anyway and, as their numbers are small (less than 10% in any organization), the manual of policies and procedures will be acceptable to 90% of the labor force, even up through several levels of higher management. So the manual is the correct thing to use in most cases.

By now you might have concluded that I am against doers. I am for them 100%, and every organization needs *some*. If the doer is known and can be placed into the proper organization with the nondoers, good effort will result. I believe these doers are valuable people who merit extra raises and should receive special consideration for any other unusual requests they may make, such as special schooling or special assignments. The trick is to know who they are and how to reward them. Many of them don't want bonuses or more money. It is good to have one or two doers in any group because they stimulate more effort from others around them. People seem to gain strength from being near them.

Doers are like yeast in bread. Just a little in every loaf is all that is needed for the whole loaf to rise. Too much in one loaf destroys it and none in another destroys that one too. Doers vitalize and activate the "loaf" they are in. Managers must first identify these people and then spread them around on the ratio of about one per ten employees, if possible. This will give good results, whatever your goal may be.

You could summarize this all in one word—*leadership*. It is as rare and precious as gold, but solid gold is too soft. In its pure state, it is mostly ornamental. It must be mixed with other less valuable metals for durability, utility, and strength. Leaders must have someone to lead.

9
The End Run

It is a characteristic of wisdom not to do desperate things.
—*Henry David Thoreau*

The end run is a dangerous maneuver on and off the playing field. In business it means going around your immediate superior to a higher authority in your organization to prove your point or gain some benefit you believe is being unjustly denied.

Most end runs fail to achieve the desired goal. As with the end run in football, the defense sees it coming and the ball carrier generally gets hit for a loss. Once in a while, when the defense is not expecting it, the end run can succeed and achieve a spectacular gain for the ball carrier.

Let us carry this analogy further into business life. First, it is not a good idea for anyone to try to run around his immediate supervisor for anything. It usually leads to a loss for the person who tried it. Even if you are "right," you violated the rules of corporate procedure and everyone above you in the chain of command gets upset with you. If you succeed, they reason you might try it again on them.

It is easy to see the end run coming, and the person who is the end runner is usually known. Bosses can defend against such actions in a variety of ways and are able to block the end run before it gets going.

In general, the reasons people consider an end run involve situations such as the following:

1. I'm due for a promotion or a raise, but my boss won't give it to me or even talk about it.
2. The department is not well run and the boss is covering it up. The higher-ups don't know, and if they did, the "fur would fly."
3. Some people in the group aren't doing their share, and the boss knows it and won't do anything about it. He gives me too much work and others not enough. He isn't interested in us or what we do.
4. I'm more competent than the boss. He knows and resents this and is afraid of me, so he holds me back and gives me poor assignments. He won't let anyone know about my good work. He is afraid I'll pass him by on the way up. He takes credit for my work.
5. There is an opportunity for new business or growth, and the boss is either unaware of it or won't do anything about it, or the client is about to cancel a contract because of serious problems.

If you try an end run for reasons 1–4, your chances of failure are more than 90%.

Superiors usually leave raises and promotions in the hands of immediate supervisors. You have little chance to ever convince a senior manager to get you a raise or promotion if your immediate supervisor says otherwise. Your best choice in situation 1 is to leave quietly and go somewhere else.

It's up to higher management to recognize and repair situation 2. If you draw attention to the fact that you know the department is poorly run, in effect, you are criticizing your boss's superiors as well. They won't like this, especially if you are correct and can prove it. So you lose both ways, whether you are right or wrong. You won't benefit.

Superiors see situation 3 as distribution of the workload on the basis of your boss's judgment of who can do more work than others. They won't interfere as long as the department's work is done on schedule and within budget. They view your department as a producing unit, and they don't look at the parts within it, as long as the department's performance is according to plan or profit goal. You may not look at it that way, but it's what they think that counts. Don't try this one; you haven't a chance of succeeding.

In situation 4, you have a slight chance of success. Higher management, on occasion, listens attentively to such situations. It is not unusual for a mediocre middle manager to hold down superior performers because he fears they may pass him by.

In such situations you may well get a hearing, but, remember, the burden of proof is on you. You better be 100% correct and be able to clearly show it to the superiors. You also had better propose what should happen to you, because replacement of the manager may create an even worse situation for you.

Let me present two examples:

Many years ago when I was fresh out of school, I was working for the government with a group of highly qualified technical people. I was a junior member and learned a lot from the nine senior members.

Our manager was a fellow in his mid-40s with more than 20 years with the organization. The senior technical people used to complain long and often about his indifference and incompetence. They thought he showed little interest in our work, wasn't available when needed, and, in general, held everyone back. They said he was holding them down.

Finally, two of the senior staff members went around end to higher management. They told their story, and about two weeks later a new manager showed up.

The new manager called a meeting, and I'll never forget the tongue lashing all of us received. The new manager had worked for our former boss on several previous projects. He liked and respected him. We were advised that our old boss had lost his wife after a lengthy illness, and he was in shock. None of us knew this, as he rarely spoke to us at all about anything.

So the new boss told us that because of the complaint received, our old boss was being transferred to a staff position until he recovered, and, in the meantime, he would be in charge. With fire in his eyes, he said if we were such "hot shots" and wanted to move ahead faster, then he would see to it that we got all the work we could handle. Believe me, he kept his promise.

The two staff members who made the end run left soon afterward, and those of us who remained felt this manager's contempt for the whole group. Fortunately, I got a transfer out about a year later, but that was, to me, an early lesson on what can happen from an end run even when you win your point.

Here's a war story to prove the point:

Our security officer in World War II served in the Army in Italy. The food was the same, day in and day out, always cooked the same, mostly stew, soup, or "C" rations.

Everyone complained about the food, so our fellow, at the urging of the others, went to the company commander. He told the captain that it was summer, and fruits and vegetables were available, so couldn't the food be better prepared? They had plenty of meat, but it was always stew and always cooked the same way.

The captain called the mess sergeant to his tent with our boy present. The captain repeated the facts of the case and said, "Sergeant, this soldier has a good suggestion. Take care of it." The end run had succeeded.

However, outside the tent the sergeant told our friend to follow him. At the mess tent was 1,000 pounds of meat. The sergeant decided that spaghetti would be nice with tossed salad. Our soldier boy agreed.

You can guess who spent the rest of the day grinding up 1,000 pounds of meat for the sauce. The dinner was a great success, but our boy could hardly lift a fork or spoon. His arms were too sore from grinding the meat and tossing the salad.

End runs are dangerous.

If you find yourself in situation 4, you had better think it through and have a definite plan of what you propose to do if you succeed in convincing higher management. There's no chance for it to work to your advantage if you remain in your former position with a replacement manager.

In situation 5, you have your best opportunity to succeed if you try the end run. However, you have to convince higher management that you have the best interests of the organization at heart first, and it has to coincide with what you want to do. There are middle managers who so concern themselves with their own department that they ignore the rest of the organization, and, at times, may even work against the interests of the larger organization while blindly pursuing the efficiency of one small part of it.

Knowing this is a real possibility, higher management generally will listen to complaints or end runs in such situations. Again, be warned, you had better be 100% right, propose a complete plan of what to do, and determine your role, if and when you get what you want.

In my career, I tried the end run only once. It succeeded, and I hurt no one because of the timing. Here's what happened:

I was part of a commercial organization that was rapidly expanding to staff up for a large, long-term government project. In such situations, the wrong people get assigned together, reorganizations go on every three months or so, and people keep getting rearranged. It can be disorganized at first. We call it the "startup blues." The larger the job, the greater the initial confusion. Most overruns occur at the beginning, but don't become obvious until near the end.

My group and I were assigned to a manager who had no knowledge of what we did. I was in charge of computer software, and my boss was an engineer. He was a fine fellow and we got along well, but he spent all his time in engineering and practically none with us.

An opportunity came up in which we could see that our client needed some additional software for a related project. When I suggested to my boss that we pursue it, he didn't react at all. Since the potential contract was for several million dollars, I felt it was in everyone's best interests for the company to pursue it.

I liked my boss. He relied on me to run the software group. He never interfered with us. He spent his entire time in his engineering group.

On the other hand, we saw an excellent business opportunity approaching. He didn't see or understand what it was. I was unable to get his interest. After much soul searching, I decided to act. I don't like the end run anyway, and here I was getting ready to do it.

Fortunately, the timing was right. Another major divisional reorganization was coming up. I went to the chief engineer and told him the story. Fortunately, he was receptive to my recommendation and together we figured out a way to do it so no one but he and I knew about it. As part of the new major organization, my department was separated from the engineering group and made an independent department with its own cost center.

The chief engineer announced it was for the purpose of overhead and billing, which was a valid reason and accepted at face value by everyone. The real reason, however, was to permit us to pursue business in the software areas. We got the new contract, and, eventually, our department grew to be larger than the group we left. In no way did we hurt my former boss, which pleased me very much. He was still there long after on other assignments.

The end run can be used when there is absolutely no other way, but it should not be used too often. I did it only once in my career, and it was successful, but I still didn't feel right in doing it. The clandestine meetings with the chief engineer and the secret plans left a bad taste in my mouth. I felt disloyal.

I would suggest that you try anything else, even leaving, before you try the end run. You may make it and score a touchdown, but if you try it more than once or twice, you are most likely to be thrown for a long loss.

10
Form versus Substance

What is your substance, whereof you are made?
—*William Shakespeare*

Form is the contour and structure of something as distinguished from its substance. Substance refers to the essence or nature of anything apart from its form.

It can be seen then that form and substance are, in effect, the opposite of each other. One (substance) is what really matters. The other (form) is the package or container that substance comes in, and should be of far less significance.

The form a message takes (written or oral, formal or informal) should be of much less significance than the content or substance of the message, but, unfortunately, in many situations, this is not so.

As managers, we deal with a great variety of subjects. In handling them, which item is of greater importance, the substance of an issue or its form? Of course, we immediately reply that substance is by far the more important, but is that where we spend most of our time? Unfortunately, some managers spend most of their time being involved with the form of an issue to the complete neglect of the substance.

Several years ago, one of our attorneys advised me that he and most of his colleagues spent approximately 85% of their legal work time on form or format, not on the true substantial issue. Guilt or innocence, right or wrong, fair or unfair, justice or injustice were not the issues that took most of the lawyer's time. Legal precedents, method of arrest, method of arraignment, legal technicalities, form of the complaint, and other trivia were the focus of most of the lawyer's efforts.

Unfortunately, business tends to be much the same. The effective manager must continually guard against being drawn into the details of format. Let your staff do these things. Lawyers, CPA's, and staff assistants will be only too happy to provide these services to free you for attention to the issues of substance, such as growth, sales, profit, long-range planning, career goals, and new technology.

The larger the organization, the more concern there is for the form of an issue rather than its substance. Procedures and policies are issued and blindly followed, whether they apply to the substance or intent of the issue.

Two examples here will illustrate the point.

At one of my former places of employment, an outside company was hired to provide guard service and other tasks. Additional duties such as raising and lowering the flag and moving the lawn sprinklers every two hours each day were part of the guard's job. All guards had clipboards with orders that listed events and the times at which they were to be done each day. This was the form or procedure.

One rainy day as I looked out the window, I saw a guard run out of the front door of our building with a raincoat on and an umbrella up. He ran over to one of the lawn sprinklers, turned it off, and moved it to the next location, according to his "order sheet." Then he turned it on again and ran back into the building. He obeyed the form and ignored the substance. He was safe in so doing because, if he made a decision that because it is raining the lawn sprinklers should be turned off to save water, he would be clearly departing from his formal orders and might be punished. He is not supposed to determine the intent or substance of orders. He just reads and obeys.

Another time I saw one of our senior programmers staggering under many pounds of computer printout that he was carrying into an engineer's office. I followed him in and asked how many pages he had. He answered, 3,000 pages. (At 3¢ per page, he had $90.00 worth of paper.)

The next day, at approximately the same time, I saw him again, staggering into the same office with another pile of paper. Again, he had over 3,000 pages of computer printout for the engineer.

Since the engineer could hardly have had time to turn over each page of his 3,000-page output from the day before, I wondered about what was going to happen to this 3,000-page output from today's computer run. My senior programmer said he didn't know or care. He was told to "run this job" once a day with certain parameters and deliver the output to this engineer. I asked him again if he knew why or what the engineer did with it. He said no, he didn't know.

I went to the engineer and asked him why he wanted this 3,000-page output each day, since clearly he could not even look at all the pages. He said he only looked at several parameters on page 50, and he didn't know why he got all the other paper. He threw it all away each day.

Someone had mixed up the form of the computer request card and checked a box that requested "full core dump and tape printout." From then on it was all automatic. No one thought about the substance or meaning of the request. Everyone followed the form of the request.

In the second case, the senior programmer should have known enough to at least question this ridiculous request. Yet, he stoutly defended himself by saying he did what he was told and "followed orders" as had the rain-soaked guard.

Of course, there are good reasons for any organization, large or small, to prepare and formalize procedures, rules, and policies, such as ensuring fair and equitable application of rules, benefits, rewards, and punishments.

The forms are intended merely to provide the method by which the substance of the issue is applied. When substance is frustrated by the thoughtless application of a form or procedure, injustice and inefficiency result.

It's all a question of judgment. A criterion of good management is knowing when to depart from the rules or policies. When, in your judgment, does the form not apply because of the substance of a particular case? Many people are unwilling to make such judgments for fear of being wrong and criticized later. It's safer to "go by the book," but a brief study of outstanding leaders or achievers in any line of work reveals that they depart from "the book" and make decisions that address the substance of the issue at hand.

As managers, you must take time away from everyday matters at least once a week to shut your office door and think about the substance and meaning of it all. It is up to each manager to determine how and on what he will spend his time. This tendency to concentrate on the form rather than the substance of an issue is by no means confined to the lower or nonmanagerial ranks. Many high-level managers and higher executives get so wrapped up in the observance of meaningless or harmful procedures that should be reversed or abandoned.

Common expressions are "don't rock the boat," or "don't make waves," or "it has never been done before." Such slogans are symptomatic of organizations that are form-oriented rather than substance-oriented. Federal, state, and local governments abound in such thinking. That is one of the reasons they tend to be inefficient and nonresponsive to the people they are supposed to serve.

Those who are aware that substance really matters, separate form from substance, and are able to affect issues of substance are the people who eventually will rise to the top in whatever profession they choose to follow and stay there.

Experts in matters of form, such as CPA's, lawyers, and financial analysts, can rise quite high in any organization, but to reach the top echelon and to remain there, you must address your efforts to matters of substance.

11
Goals

Never let yourself be trammeled by the bonds of orthodoxy; always think for yourself and remember the herd is usually wrong.
—Attributed to General A. P. Wavell

Most of us want to live our lives to the fullest and do the best we can for ourselves, for those we love, and for society in general. This requires that we first decide what it is we want to do and next, what to do to reach our goal.

Most people, however, have no real goals or plans, and that is why they never reach any goal. If you don't set a goal, then you drift through life and let others decide for you what you do, how, where, and when. You react to events rather than cause them to happen.

Let us consider the steps necessary to establish a goal and the intermediate plans needed to reach the goal.

1. *Write your career plan.* A written plan may seem obvious, but most people do not make one.

For young people starting out fresh from school or college, it is important to know what you want to do in life. Unfortunately, many just don't know. Grabbing the first job one can find after graduation may be an economic necessity, but it will lead to disappointment, frustration, or worse later on if it does not fit into the long-range desires or career goals of the person involved.

Make a five-year plan and then work back to the present time. State what you want five years from now. Next, what do you want one year from now? Then determine what to do next week to advance toward your goals.

It is difficult enough to make good plans come to reality. It is almost impossible to succeed if you have no goals or no plans to reach them. Do it now. If you can't do it alone, then get help.

2. *Review your plan at least once a year.* Any plan is a prediction of the future. Naturally, no one can accurately predict what events will occur or how. It is necessary then to review and, if necessary, modify or update goals.

We may find that we are not on our career plan. What we hoped to do didn't get done. It's time then to evaluate and reassess our position or perhaps even our goals.

A written career plan is much like a navigation chart one draws before starting on a long boat trip. We must determine where we are in respect to where we planned to be. Adjustments are always necessary. We alter our present course to get back to our original course, or sometimes we find we either want or have to change some short-range goals that are now impossible to achieve. Sometimes we find we must postpone or abandon some desired interim goal or primary goals. It is good to have alternative goals in some order of priority if we find we are unable to reach our first-priority goal.

This should not cause alarm unless you always must abandon your goals because you never reach any. In that event, some outside help is necessary because either you are making completely unrealistic goals for yourself or, if the goals are reasonable and within reach, you don't know how to achieve them.

Don't be afraid or embarrassed to ask for help. Most managers are willing to help. That doesn't mean you charge into your boss's office with complaints about your work, or co-workers, or other such problems.

A serious talk with your boss about where you want to go

and when is good for both you and your boss. If you find the boss doesn't want to do this, then you might consider seeking a new boss, because your present boss may not be a good manager.

Not enough employees ever do this. I don't know why, unless they are afraid of what they may hear about themselves. During my career, I have reassigned and transferred people into other jobs when they told me what they wanted to do. I was more than happy to do this, as most managers are, if we only can know what the person wants to do.

Don't overdo this sort of thing. Once every year or so is sufficient. Coming in every two or three months for guidance leads the boss to believe you need too much help and are not ready for a promotion to manage other people. Let me cite a couple of examples.

Some years ago, we hired a senior computer programmer. In a short while he proved his ability and value to our organization, so I called him in to tell him so and give him a raise. He told me that at his former place of employment no one had ever done this. He said he never received a raise in the four years he had worked there. When I asked why, he said that each year his immediate supervisor recommended him for a merit raise, but each time it was rejected by higher management. He said the reason he never got a raise was his supervisor's boss had him mixed up with someone else and, as a result, any raise request was automatically turned down.

I asked him why he put up with it for four years. He replied that he never asked the reason for being refused each year because he was afraid to cause trouble. It was only after he had resigned that he found the courage to go up the line and find out. It was all a mistake, but he let it go on for four long years. He received profuse apologies from all concerned.

I told him, in my opinion, it was mostly his fault that it had gone on. He disagreed and blamed his management for the error. Regardless of who was at fault, he let it happen to him because he had no plan and no courage to ask a legitimate question about his own career advancement.

The second case involved an excellent woman programmer. She was so good at one particular aspect of the work that she was constantly directed into a narrow, specialized area because she did it so well.

She told her immediate supervisor that she wanted to work on other types of problems so she could gain a variety of experience and move ahead on her career plan. Her supervisor ignored her requests, because keeping her in her one special area made his job easier for him.

She came to me (with permission from her manager) and explained her situation and her career goals. I transferred her to another assignment. Today she is one of our senior managers, doing what she likes. She is a good technical manager. Her salary and position have passed that of her former supervisor and rightly so.

So you see the value of having a plan and speaking up when someone or something is standing in the way of reaching your goals.

Now let's proceed to some specific day-to-day techniques. The following suggestions are a combination of my own experiences as a manager plus those of many other managers with whom I have discussed these topics.

3. *Get into work early; out of work late.* Most people don't like clock watchers. They make everybody nervous and they give the distinct impression that they can't wait to be elsewhere.

Getting into work early, or on time, or late is just a habit. Most bosses like to see people come into work a bit early.

Arriving early can only help your career because bosses like to see this habit in their employees.

Many managers will put up with a lot more from employees who have a history of being early to work than from the others. Most managers believe that a prompt employee is automatically a good employee. If you should cause a problem or make a mistake at work, then the boss will discount it somewhat if you are an early arriver.

As for staying a bit late at work once in a while, the same advice applies. It is next to impossible to come to a logical breakpoint in our work at the same time each day. The managers like to see employees, on occasion, finish what they are doing before they leave for the day.

It is most disconcerting for a manager to see people rushing to get out of the building promptly at 4:45 P.M. each day. What's the rush? Do they hate their work that much? Is working a bit late out of the question? Aren't these the same people who come in to work late each morning? These are some of the thoughts that cross the boss's mind as he watches the daily exodus.

Stay a little late once in a while if you want to get ahead in your career more than you want to get out of the company parking lot each day.

4. *Wear a smile.* Everyone likes to see a cheerful face now and then. There's enough gloom in the world outside, so make it a point to be cheerful with your co-workers and especially the boss.

Most managers spend a lot of their time dealing with unhappy customers, schedule slippages, cost overruns, late budget reports, and personnel problems. They rarely see a calm, happy face.

Let them see a smile on yours and hear a pleasant greeting from you. It will do wonders for you.

Where I work, guards check badges as we enter. At one

entrance was a young woman who checked each badge with a smile and a pleasant word for everyone.

One day when we came in, she wasn't there. The new guard was a grouch who just pushed the button to unlock the door. Everyone wondered what happened to the girl and we all asked about her.

We found out she had been promoted. We were pleased for her, but we missed her pleasant face each morning. We were all ready to go to the management in her behalf if she had been reassigned or let go.

Smile and get the promotion. Frown and stay where you are.

5. *Don't complain or argue.* The chronic complainer exists in every organization. But he doesn't go far. Bosses and co-workers turn you off like a radio with too much static and never listen to you again once you get the reputation of being a chronic complainer.

Managers are reluctant to promote such people because complainers think they got promoted because they complained.

No one is indispensable. There are usually any number of qualified men or women who can do the job well, so why not promote someone who is pleasant?

6. *Admit your mistakes.* If you make decisions, it is only natural that sooner or later you will do something wrong. When this occurs, it is best if you are the first to tell your boss before he finds it out from other sources.

A good boss may be a bit upset but, after he or she calms down, a boss realizes you are being honest. The boss will appreciate your honesty and you too. If your boss becomes so angry when you make an honest mistake that you are afraid to tell the truth, then I strongly suggest that you find another job.

Managers want and rely on people who do their best

and admit their mistakes. People who are promoted generally come from the ranks of the reliable, even if they aren't the smartest.

7. *Seek additional responsibility at work.* Good managers like to see initiative in subordinates; poor managers do not. So it is always to your advantage to do your job to the best of your ability, and if you get it done early, tell your manager and ask for more responsibility or more work.

If the manager ignores you, tells you to "cool it," or piles too much added work on you to teach you a lesson, then you have a poor manager, and a new job elsewhere is in order for you.

Usually, however, in such a situation, the manager will most certainly take notice of you and mark you down as someone to watch.

As one progresses up the ladder in any line of business, a job becomes less well defined, and more responsibility is placed on one's shoulders. Only people with initiative and judgment can function in such ill-defined areas. The sooner you demonstrate to your managers that you have such initiative and desire for additional responsibility, the sooner you will get your chance. Most managers are more than willing to give you the opportunities you want. There are some good reasons for this.

First, the manager knows that he or she should push responsibility and decision-making authority as far down the line or as near to the action as possible. This has a twofold beneficial effect. The manager is training those down the line to develop managerial skills in an area of work with which they are familiar. This is necessary before they move on into other areas in which they will be less sure of themselves. It's training for advancement.

Also, the more responsibility and decision making the manager gives to those below, the more time the senior person has for other work and planning. The higher one goes, the less one deals in the present and the more one plans for the future.

Usually, managers who hold all decisions and authority to themselves believe no one below in the organization is capable of taking over. That's not good for any subordinate.

Don't be afraid to ask the boss for additional responsibility when you think you are ready for it. You might be pleasantly surprised.

8. *Disagree if you want, but do what the boss says.* No matter how often you hear managers say they don't want "yes men" around them, the fact is they like to be agreed with and they don't like to be told they are wrong or that you don't agree with them.

This leads us now into the delicate area of disagreement with the boss. This problem calls for judgment. Here are a few tips on how to do it and how not to do it.

First, let's consider how not to disagree. Assume the boss tells you to do a job in a certain way, which you are sure is wrong. You have more knowledge and experience on the job, and the boss is rusty or out of date. Don't ignore the boss and do it your way. Even if later events prove you to be right, the boss will be embarrassed and will remember it for a long time, probably to your disadvantage. If you ignore the boss and later are proved wrong, you must face the unhappy consequences. You can't win either way if you ignore the boss's orders.

Another wrong way is to lie to the boss by saying you agree but then proceed to do it another way.

Another wrong approach is to forget about it and see what happens. Several years ago, I had a secretary who was excellent in all respects except that she had memory lapses when I asked her to do something she didn't want to do. After several discussions about this problem, all to no avail, I solved the problem by having a memory lapse of my own. One payday I had the payroll clerk give me the secretary's paycheck, and I told her I forgot where I put it. The next day, I told her my memory had failed as I handed the frantic lady her check. It was harsh medicine, but she never again had a memory lapse. I don't think what I did was right, even though it was effective, and I wouldn't do it today.

What does one do when one disagrees with the boss? First, tell the boss that you don't think what he or she wants to do is correct and explain why. Then explain how you think it should be done. This should be done in private, of course, to permit the boss to "save face." Such statements as "It won't work," or "I disagree" don't help much if that's all you have to say. Give your reasons.

The boss may agree with you and do it your way; if so, all well and good. The boss may, however, insist on his or her original orders being carried out. In this case, do it exactly as the boss has instructed. Tell no one else you disagree, and do it quickly and to the best of your ability. The boss will watch you carefully to see what you do. If you act promptly on his or her orders, this is a big plus for you, because the boss knows how hard it was for you to carry out an order with which you disagreed. In the long run, it matters little who was right. What matters is that the boss knows you will do your job, even under difficult circumstances.

It is your immediate supervisor who gets you your pay raises and gives you the opportunities for promotion and advancement. Everyone likes to work with or for a person who can be relied upon to do the work and not have disagreements affect the performance.

In some cases, you may not be able to express your

honest opinions to your boss. If this is so, I recommend that you get another job, because this is not a healthy working environment for anyone. The choice, of course, is up to you if you are in such circumstances.

A word of caution is in order here, however. I am not talking about doing anything illegal, immoral, or against your conscience or beliefs. In no case should anyone do things or carry out orders that he or she believes are wrong in a moral or legal sense. No one admires a person who sells out his or her conscience or morals for advancement or monetary reward.

I am discussing those nonmoral issues that arise every day in any business or organization. Let your boss know what you think, but do what the boss says when the discussions are over. You might do well here to consider that the boss's instructions are orders to be carried out, not a premise upon which to start a debate or a discussion. The boss may not always be right, but he or she is always the boss.

9. *Compliment others freely and often.* Passing out excessive, insincere compliments labels one as an insincere person.

What we recommend here is well-intentioned and well-deserved praise for a job well done. Appreciation for work well done is almost as necessary as good pay. A compliment or a thank you now and then helps build and sustain morale.

Always look for legitimate opportunities to praise someone for an extra or successful effort. People will want to work with you and for you when they know their efforts are appreciated.

Don't take the credit for anyone else's ideas or work. It can only temporarily benefit your career, because sooner or later it will be discovered, and no one will want to work with or for you. I know of no way to shut off cooperation more quickly or permanently than to try to ride on someone else's coattails, or to take credit for someone else's work.

These recommendations are by no means an all-inclusive list of things to do. They are, however, common to all lines of work, and putting them into practice can advance your career.

12
Human Behavior in the Organization

It's a funny thing about life. If you refuse to accept
anything but the best, you very often get it.
—*Somerset Maugham*

The single most important factor in anyone's career advancement or lack of it is, in my opinion, his or her behavior patterns or attitudes displayed at work. Most career preparation concentrates almost exclusively on the technical aspects of the jobs to be done. Courses in the behavioral sciences should be required for all those majoring in business administration, engineering, and mathematics.

It may well be, as some experts testify, that a person's behavior pattern or approach to life is so set, even before he or she enters first grade, that it is useless to try to teach or improve anyone in this area. The idea seems to be that whatever approach to life the person has received through either heredity or environment, or both, it's too late to try to cope with it or too difficult to try to change anyone after the age of five or six. This may or may not be true, but I can testify, from some years of experience as a manager at various levels in several large organizations, that it is very difficult, if not impossible, to change undesirable behavior patterns in adults.

Since those in business generally deal with adults, our discussion on behavior and attitudes will be restricted to adults.

Let us consider some examples. The word *secretary* is a

derivative of the word secret. Most secretaries handle company-sensitive material such as payrolls, accounts receivable, the boss's personal and corporate correspondence. Many secretaries have authority to open the boss's mail, read it, and pass on to the boss what the secretary thinks is important. They also prepare outgoing letters. In short, the secretary is privy to the inner workings of the company at the highest level. The most common reason for dismissing secretaries is that they talk too much about company business to people who have no right to know it. Many secretaries can't keep *secrets*.

Personality problems were the cause in 89% of the cases in which naval and civilian personnel were demoted, discharged, reassigned, or passed over for promotion, according to a government personnel expert. The persons concerned either would not do the job, had bad work habits, or argued with superiors, peers, or subordinates. These people had behavior problems that wrecked their careers. My own experiences have convinced me that in nine out of ten cases, most problems with employees concern chronic lateness, too much time on the telephone, leaving work early, arguing with others, refusal to obey legitimate orders from their bosses, or arguing with a customer. These are behavior problems. They have little, if anything, to do with the person's ability. Behavior problems, even of a very immature nature, exist among even the most educated people.

What can management do when it detects unacceptable behavior in employees? One of the largest companies in the United States has an unusual approach. Each year 50 or so recent MBA graduates enter this company's management training program. After vigorous training and testing, the few survivors (5 to 10) are then put into the corporate management structure. They generally develop long and successful careers at the company.

The courses given, the training and testing, however sophisticated, are based on the principle that all persons tend to repeat themselves in whatever behavior pattern they show early in their careers. People rarely change one way or the other. The risk takers will continue to take risks. The decision makers will make decisions. The cautious ones remain cautious. Indecisive people will stay indecisive.

The success of this big management training course lay in detecting the built-in behavior or reaction patterns of trainees, assigning them to positions that required the type of behavior they exhibited early in the program, and then relying on their not changing their patterns of behavior in future corporate life. The company concluded it is pointless to try to change any person's behavior. Change the jobs to fit the behavior, and you have the best chance of success. Accept people as they are when they join the company.

Only the largest of companies can afford to hire 50 top MBA graduates each year and spend four to five years to get only 5 or 10 of the best to stay on and earn back for the company the large cash outlay required for such an operation.

Those of us in smaller organizations can, however, learn something from this. We should not try to change any person's behavior pattern. The failure rate is too high. We should try, whenever possible, to reassign or transfer people into areas of work that fit their desires and in which they can function effectively and without pressure. For example, some people like to work with other people, and some do not. Some people like routine work; some find it dull. Some like research work in which everything is new and always changing, and some just can't work in such an environment. There are no guidelines to work from, and some people can't stand the uncertainty. All of this has little, if anything, to do with intelligence, training, or education. It is in the basic makeup of the person that was set in place long before he or she ever applied for work.

Often, just by asking people what type of work they prefer, we can make a fit. When unable to obtain a match, or if the person repeats unacceptable behavior on two assignments of a different nature with different people, I suggest that termination is the best solution, and the sooner the better for all concerned.

13
Indecision

Most people have to be led; some have to be driven, but few, very few have to be restrained.
—*General George Patton*

Indecision has wrecked more careers early or in midstream than any other single personal characteristic, according to a consensus of senior personnel.

Most people who rise to the top in their chosen careers share a common characteristic: they are decisive. They make decisions and they aren't afraid to take risks. When it's time to do something, they do it, while others stand around and wait for someone else to act.

History is replete with stories of people who achieved great goals by making decisions they had no business making or in rising to the occasion when the situation demanded that someone act. The decision maker forged ahead, did what he or she thought best, and stood ready to pay the consequences one way or the other.

In the survey questionnaire of senior executives in business, question 38 asked, "What single factor do you consider most significant in preventing a subordinate from rising higher in your organization?" Sixty-five percent of the respondents said, *indecisiveness.*

Among reasons that many people are indecisive are fear of the unknown, fear of making a mistake and being proved wrong, and fear of any change.

There is not much that anyone can do one way or the

88

other about a person who lacks the will to make decisions. We can train just about any willing person with reasonable intelligence to do most jobs. Intellectual ability or lack of it seldom seems to be the problem in limiting one's advancement.

Indecision seems to be a built-in emotional or automatic knee jerk response to any unexpected situations the person encounters. The indecisive person often is unaware that he or she is indecisive.

Any good manager, supervisor, or military officer will tell you that the place he or she is needed most is where the problems are or the action is. In football, he's called the middle linebacker or free safety man, who follows the action and reacts to the situation as it unfolds before him. You cannot train anyone to do this. He just knows when to rush in, or slide out sideward, or drop back to anticipate the pass. He must anticipate, decide, and act because if he waits to see where the ball goes before he makes his move, then it is too late.

Coaches will tell you it is difficult, if not impossible, to teach this sort of thing. It is either there in the fellow or it's not. If not, then get another one. If it's there, then it can be refined, polished, and improved upon.

Decisive people can and do make mistakes. In fact, they make more mistakes than others because they do more things than the others. When a decision maker lacks intelligence, the organization has a truly dangerous person, one who lacks ability or judgment. They are quite rare, but when identified they should be removed from their position as soon as possible.

What you are much more likely to encounter is the hard-working, intelligent, dedicated subordinate or superior who performs well and deserves some advancement but tends to be indecisive. When given the next higher position, such a person starts to "drop the ball" because the job calls for decisions and the indecisive one doesn't make them in time or at all. They become afraid and too cautious. Since they don't make decisions, things happen to them (someone else is deciding for them). Such people spend their time reacting to events rather than acting and controlling the events.

The person has the education, training, experience, and ability to function in a decision-making capacity, but suddenly you notice things going wrong, schedules slipping, cost overruns occurring, and other problems that are common to the indecisive manager. It never seems to be entirely his or her fault. Things seems to just not work out. It's up to higher management to move with speed then because a replacement is in order.

Once one makes a decision, then it can be reviewed, discussed, and evaluated by higher authority, and a judgment can be made of the manager's performance. This may very well be the reason that some won't or hesitate to make a decision. The reasoning seems to be that no one can get you for something you didn't do. "Don't rock the boat" is the classic line of reasoning of an indecisive person.

Only about 10% of any group of people have the ability and desire to exercise any decision-making authority. In the smaller organization in which senior managers know just about everyone in the group, it is fairly easy to spot those who will make decisions and those who won't.

In the larger organizations, it is much more difficult, and the effects are more serious and far-reaching. Things happen or don't, and no one knows who did or didn't do it, or why. Rumors and counter rumors fly all over the office or factory. No one seems to know what's going on or where they are supposed to go. Someone hasn't made any decisions or plans, and it shows up and down the line.

I have seen an organization that was, in reality, directed

and run by the manager's secretary, who was a very decisive person, and the boss was not. She ran the organization
through her boss. He would react to her opinions and
decisions. She became progressively more bold to the
point that she started giving the engineers and scientists
direct orders on her own. It was amazing to see how often
she was right.

It was only when the higher technical personnel reacted
against her direct manner, which they found offensive,
that something was done. If she had developed some tact,
she could have continued on, but she lost out because she
forgot she was still a secretary and had no business being
actively involved in the bosses' decision-making process. I
think she alone could have managed the group. She had
been doing it rather well for some time. Her downfall was
not that she made decisions; it was her lack of tact in the
way she chose to implement them.

It was all the fault of the boss, a nice guy who wouldn't
hurt anyone, but his indecisiveness resulted in many hurt
feelings, transfers, arguments (the secretary left), and
other unfortunate reactions that could well have been
avoided if the boss had only made his own decisions in the
first place.

Now that we have discussed some of the consequences
of indecision, what can be done about it? I don't think
much can be done about indecisive people; it seems to be
part of their emotional makeup. But there are things that
each of us should do so we can recognize when we are
dealing with someone who is indecisive. If you are placed
below such a person in your organization, he or she will
slow your career advancement, because the group to
which you belong won't perform well in the long run, and
all tend to suffer when you work with or for a loser.

Indecisive people below you in the organization can in-
hibit your career advancement too by fouling up whatever

section or group they manage. You, as the senior manager, must assume full responsibility for this failure, because you are responsible for what your subordinates do. Such people also require a disproportionate amount of their supervisors' time because they look anywhere for help when it comes to decision-making time.

Indecisiveness is an incurable ailment, so let's look at the symptoms and prognosis. One telltale sign is that many indecisive people imitate for its own sake. I have seen some go so far as to dress like other managers just to be like them. When asked why they do things in a certain way, they say because the others are doing it that way. They don't want to do it their own way. It may be different, and they don't want to be different.

A decisive person makes plans both in personal life and in the workplace. If your boss or subordinate doesn't plan out the work and actively direct its progress, he or she is showing one of the classic signs of indecision. If one doesn't know what is going on or what one is supposed to do, then one can't be expected to make decisions. In order to make decisions, one has to have some sort of plan or goal; otherwise, on what basis are the decisions to be made? How does one judge success or failure?

A decisive person is not afraid to take a risk or to seek change. If he or she usually has to wait for more information before deciding on a course of action, that may be just his or her way of postponing the decision point. One rarely has all the information one wants or needs to make proper decisions.

Many times one has to estimate the situation or, in other words, make a guess and be right or wrong. It is a decision point and the decision should be made. If it is later proved wrong, then make another decision to correct the first one. For some people this is virtually impossible to do. The least doubt or uncertainty stops them. If the boss or subordinate doesn't make decisions on time, then this too is a bad sign. He or she is indecisive.

Decision makers are not afraid to put their decisions on record for later judgment or evaluation. They should have enough confidence so as not to be afraid if others know what they decide. If they always want to know first what you think but rarely tell you what they think, that is a sign of lack of self-confidence.

There's a story about President Lincoln and a cabinet meeting during the Civil War. Mr. Lincoln had to find a new commander for the Union Army. He was having trouble with indecisive Army commanders.

Mr. Lincoln presented the name of his choice for the new commander to the cabinet for discussion. After much debate, he called for a vote. The twelve cabinet members voted no. Mr. Lincoln announced the results of the ballot: "twelve no's and one aye, the aye's have it." Mr. Lincoln, who voted yes, was telling his cabinet members that their votes were advisory only. He was the decision maker, not them.

If your superiors, peers, or subordinates continually form or join committees to run things, those persons may be indecisive. Committees should not be given decision-making power except under unusual and temporary circumstances. Committees serve best when they collect information and serve as advisors to the decision makers.

The problem now is what to do if you must deal with an indecisive person. You may find it acceptable to stay if you are indecisive yourself. If so, keep a watch on who really runs things. Make friends with that person because you are going to rise or fall as he does. You may need this person later on in your career because you will probably always need someone else to help you.

If you are the decisive type, two courses of action are open to you. You can get out of the place you are in and go to work for an intelligent decision maker. It is hoped by now that you can recognize one who is and one who isn't.

If it is not possible for you to leave the job, then you might opt to become the power behind the throne. You could play the role of the leader through the less decisive superior. This calls for tact and the type of office politics that can often be fatal if one stumbles, but many have survived and grown in such situations for long periods of time. It is my opinion, however, that the true decision maker doesn't stay too long in that situation.

In conclusion, then, those with the desire, ability, and opportunity to exercise leadership roles with decision-making responsibility can rise in any organization.

14
Interviews and Résumés

Time but the impression deeper makes, as streams their channels deeper wear. —*Robert Burns*

Employment interviews are essential to getting the job you want. Interviews are also a part of reassignment within an organization. But an important preliminary to an interview is a résumé, which is presented in advance. A résumé serves a function similar to the introduction to a book. If the introduction captures interest, then one reads the rest of the book. If the résumé makes a good impression, an employer grants an interview to find out more about a job applicant.

The most common mistake that most job applicants make is to write only one standard résumé and use it over and over again with no changes or variations. They have many copies made and flood the market with the same résumé in hopes it will bring the desired results. Except in unusual circumstances, this will not get you what you want. You leave it to the reader to decide what, if anything, in your résumé is applicable to the company or the job in question. This places a burden on someone who must read many résumés every day.

Another common mistake made in résumés is the use of cryptic or "buzz" words to describe your experience in sentences that are too short to mean anything, unless the reader knows exactly what you have been doing.

I remember a résumé from a senior programmer who

described five years of experience as follows: "Worked on APACHE and MOBILE APACHE equipment." That was all for five years of work. Fortunately for him, I knew he was a computer programmer who wrote software for Atlas Program Checkout Equipment (APACHE) and a later version that was placed in a truck for mobility. I was also familiar with the particular program; otherwise, what he wrote would have meant nothing.

If your résumé contains a transcript of your college grades, attach a key to help decipher grades such as 2.75, 3.014, or 1.73. Most managers are more familiar with the A, B, C, D grades. Also, numbers such as 100% or 85% are easily understood. Colleges have changed to different methods of listing grades, and, as they vary from school to school, many senior managers don't understand them. Many applicants assume that because they understand them, then everyone else will.

Special honors or awards also should be explained. Stating you were president of the ΔΔΔ Society means nothing, unless you describe what it is.

Write or type your résumé neatly, with your name and address at the top. Put a date on it, too, so the recipient will know when it was prepared. Next, list your educational background with degrees earned and honors awarded. Books or articles that you published come next, but don't list them all if you have more than 10 or so. In that case, attach a separate page and list them under publications.

As for your work experience, start with your current position and work backward in time. List dates, name of supervisor, reason for leaving, and then describe each job in some specific detail.

A résumé should not be more than two or three pages in length.

It is important that you tailor each résumé toward the particular position you are seeking. This means you should emphasize that portion of your background, training, or education that is pertinent to the desired job. If, for example, you seek a job in accounting, then your training and experience in accounting and related business areas should be emphasized and other expertise given lesser attention.

The general résumé that is run off on a copying machine does not receive as much attention as the personal letter and résumé that is specially prepared and typed and sent to an individual. This usually gets a response.

Our company has a rule that any letter or résumé that is sent to an individual by name will receive a personal response. Mimeographed copies of résumés do not get any response. We get far too many and most do not apply to the kind of work we do. Anyone responding to want ads and firing off résumés to 100 places in hopes of getting a response is taking a long shot.

Next, consider to whom you should send the résumé or with whom you should make contact. The best approach is a personal one. Do you know anyone in the target company? If so, start there. That person can advise you whom to contact and how. If you don't know anyone there, I suggest you contact the top person in the target company. Many people are afraid to do this, but it often produces results.

Speaking from personal experience, I got a desired transfer when I was working for the government by writing directly to the chief scientist of a research laboratory after several unsuccessful attempts to get a job there by going through the personnel department. I tried for six months through personnel. The letter to the chief scientist resulted in my receiving a telephone call; an interview followed, and I was on the job in six weeks.

So, make your initial approach to the highest level you can, but be sure you get his or her name to make it a personal contact. Do your homework and learn what the company does. In your typewritten letter, show some knowledge of the company's work and how your background prepares you for the particular job you are seeking.

You want your letter and résumé to so impress the top man or woman that he or she will direct it to someone in the organization for a reply. You can be sure you will get a response, because the branch manager or whoever receives the résumés from the boss will certainly respond to avoid discourtesy to the boss.

Remember, the reason for all this is to get to see someone, so you can convince him to hire you. You will win or lose the job at the interview. Letters and résumés only prepare the way, but they must be well done with the end in view of getting to see someone who can hire you.

Now, you have an interview coming up and an application to fill out. Fill it out neatly (preferably, get it typed). Neatness counts here, because you are now showing how careful you are and how well you can follow simple instructions. If you can't fill out an application form correctly, you can't be too interested in the job, no matter what experience you have. Take time and care to do it properly.

An example here can prove my point. At one of my former places of employment, we were reviewing a young lady's résumé and job application. On the application form were questions about experience, degrees earned, publications, memberships in technical or professional organizations, and awards or honors received. (This of course refers to such honors as class valedictorian, awards for professional excellence, and honor societies.

This young lady wrote in the awards and honors received section, "I was elected beauty queen of the senior prom." While we all enjoyed that (it provided conversation around the coffee machine), she received a polite form letter in reply, and we never saw this beauty.

Now, you have passed two hurdles and you come to the personal interview. Here is where most people make the fatal mistakes. Everything up to this point was done so you could talk your way into the job. Here are a few hints on what to do and what not to do at the interview.

1. Be prompt or even a little early (15 minutes early), but not so early as to appear desperate for the job and too concerned. If for any reason you are late, call up and postpone the interview, but get another interview appointment.

Remember the manager's point of view. If you are late for the interview, then he or she will immediately conclude that you'll be a chronic latecomer to work. Most managers prefer a person of average ability who is prompt and willing over a brighter employee who does things late or in a sloppy manner. Lateness reveals careless attitude.

2. Be neat. You have every right to dress as you please, but remember the boss's point of view. Those in authority, too, have rights to their own opinions and preferences. The boss knows he or she can't refuse to hire you because he or she doesn't like your clothes or long hair. However, the boss will find some other "valid" reason to not hire you that is socially and legally acceptable.

3. Do your research about the company. Know its product or purpose. Tell the manager what you plan or want to do and, if possible, how. Let him or her ask the questions.

4. Know the salary you want and don't be afraid to state it. If you say, "I'll take whatever you think I'm worth or what everyone else gets," you are showing anxiety and indicating weakness.

5. Don't overestimate your importance either. One young fellow I interviewed several years ago wanted $25,000 a year as a starting salary. I asked him how he

arrived at this figure, since he was fresh out of a little-known college, with only fair grades and no experience. He said that was what his friends told him he should get. I told him to go and get it from them. That was the end of the interview.

6. Don't be a know-it-all. No one is indispensable, and no one likes an overconfident person at a job interview. If you appear overconfident at the interview, the manager concludes that you would be insufferable once you came to work.

7. Be yourself. Don't try to imitate anyone else.

8. Don't crack jokes or use snappy sayings. You may be a laugh riot around the coffee machine later, but don't try it at the job interview. The person to whom you are speaking is looking for a mature, hard-working person, not a comedian. Don't get funny until after you are hired, and then be funny only when the boss isn't around.

9. Don't come in with a sob story about how much you need the job or what troubles you have at your current job. Employers do not hire people with problems. Some have enough problems with the people already there and don't need any more.

Another practice to consider, because it is gaining in popularity, is the *stress interview*. Usually, the interviewer does his or her best to put you at ease. An interviewer usually smiles, gets you a cup of coffee, and chats briefly to relax you.

The stress interview is designed to test your reactions to stress if the job for which you are applying involves stress or strain. If you are being interviewed for a manager's position in which you will be under pressure, then the interviewer tries to apply some pressure at the interview.

The interviewer may ask provocative questions and watch you to see if you get upset and how you react. One interviewer had his secretary call him on the telephone about every five or ten minutes or so during the interview to disrupt the conversation. The interviewer would dash from the room once or twice for several minutes and return and say to the hapless person being interviewed, "Where were we?" What if you forget what was being discussed?

Such tactics are designed to put pressure on you to see how you react. The idea is to try to put you in the type of working environment you may be in after you get the job. If you blow up or get flustered, you are out.

I don't approve of this new technique, but it is gaining in popularity, so you should be aware that it may happen to you. Keep it in the back of your mind, so you can recognize it and react coolly.

15
Layoffs

"What is better than presence of mind in a disaster?"
"Absence of body."   —Punch

A layoff is a disaster, similar to an accident, fire, flood, earthquake, or plague. In a dismissal, forced termination, or firing, at least one of the parties involved wants it to happen. But no one wants a layoff.

Consider the mass layoff. Hundreds or possibly thousands of people are all let go in a relatively short period of time (several weeks or a few months). They flood the market looking for jobs. Some even form groups and meet once a week to socialize and comfort each other in their mutual distress. You may feel better when you meet your fellow victims, but you are treating the effects, not the cause of the problem.

Several years ago, a large newspaper in the Midwest closed, and everyone was let go. Recently, I read that the former employees have started to hold annual conventions on the anniversary date of their layoff with a banquet and speakers.

From involvement in a mass layoff, there are lessons to be learned. Many are predictable.

When a contemplated layoff of a large number of people is in the offing, a great deal of planning has to go on within the company, and the following symptoms begin to appear:

1. The company is concerned about its corporate image

and starts to hold secret high-level meetings to figure out how to conduct the layoff. If you are high up enough in the organization or have relatives or friends who are, then, secret or not, the word leaks out.

2. If the layoff plan reaches the plant level so that managers whom you work for get the word, they start to act differently. Sworn to secrecy, they avoid contact with their people now, or become less concerned about regular daily chores. They are preoccupied with worry about their own careers.

3. Some resignations of key personnel start to occur as those in the know look out for themselves and leave before the mass exodus. A sudden increase in departures of senior or key personnel is an early warning sign of what is coming.

4. Strangely, like a final battle just before the surrender, a business often goes into heavy overtime and becomes very busy just before the mass layoff.

The reason for such an overtime push is that the company is rushing to completion of a big contract, which is overdue and probably over budget. The company wants to get the job done so as to cut its losses and close the plant as soon as possible. If you observe the concentration of most or all of your organization's resources on one job, that is another early warning signal.

5. As rumors start to fly, higher management decides that the general manager, chief engineer, or some senior person should deny the rumor publicly. Either an announcement is sent out to everyone or a meeting is held with department managers, at which a spokesperson denies the rumor and makes general statements, followed by a morale-building lecture. If you carefully listen to or read the statements, you generally can see the layoff coming.

The spokesperson may announce, "No matter what false rumors you hear, we are not going to close down."

That may be true, but what about the layoff or reduction in force? This is not mentioned. Look for what they don't say rather than what they do say.

6. Internal company transfers start to rise as people move away from the threatened business area and onto a more secure project. Friends try to help each other by getting each other desired transfers and relocations in time.

7. Strangely (again, like an army on the verge of surrender), the bureaucratic functions continue to operate on their own inertia. Merit raises, promotions, and other functions proceed as if nothing were wrong. I well remember a friend being promoted to a manager's position and two weeks later being laid off along with hundreds of others. We scarcely had time to celebrate his promotion before he was out looking for another job.

If other pre-conditions exist that indicate a layoff is in the offing, don't be reassured that it can't be true because someone receives a promotion or annual salary increases just went into effect last week.

These things have nothing to do with the causes or effects of a general layoff. They will happen anyway. Some operations are so big that you can "pull the plug" and they won't stop for weeks or months. They start up and run down according to their own bureaucratic time schedule. They seem to have a life of their own.

If you observe some of these early signs that a big layoff is on the way, you can take some steps to protect yourself and maybe later help a few others as well.

If you believe that a layoff is on the way, the first decision you have to make is whether to stay with the organization or not. If not, move quickly to get another job before the market is flooded and everyone is looking for the same type of job you want. If you are ever the victim of an accident in which there are many injured, it's best to arrive at the hospital very early when there are many doctors and nurses available to treat you, rather than arrive later when there are patients all over the halls and no doctors or nurses available at all.

I have witnessed many people, who saw a layoff coming, sit in place and let it hit them, department by department, in large numbers, as the system dismissed them in order according to a week-by-week layoff list. I watched them panic, cry, and rage against the system when they got the pink slip. Yet, they quietly sat and waited for it to come, knowing it was coming. I don't know why people do this, but I don't recommend waiting and doing nothing.

I was involved in a layoff in late 1962, in which all the pre-conditions described here existed. The chief engineer at a meeting for managers and senior engineers delivered the usual denial of layoff rumors.

I immediately went to my boss and asked him for the truth. He said he couldn't talk about it, because he was sworn to secrecy. So I asked a direct question: "Do you think I should look for another position as soon as I can?" He answered, "Yes."

I immediately put out feelers for another position and soon got one. I gave my notice, and the layoff started later that week. After arriving at my new job, I was able to recruit 16 talented people for my new employer during the next two months. This helped my career, because I was made a department manager to handle this new group.

I was no more technically talented than the others. I just got there first, because I observed the warning signals and acted. Others either did not observe the same signals that I did, or they chose not to do anything about it.

Let us now discuss what you can do if you want to stay with the company and survive the layoff. Why would anyone want to do this and stay during and after a layoff? There are several good reasons.

1. Unless the company is going bankrupt, it will eventually recover. Executives will work hard to restore former sales and profit. Anyone who can help in this situation will receive greater than usual advancement and raises. The opportunity exists for rapid double jumps in the career patterns.

During or immediately after any large layoff, a wave of resignations takes place. These come from people the company wants to keep for the recovery, but who become discouraged as many friends and co-workers leave.

If you have to reduce the staff by 200, it's best to lay off 150 and wait for the resignations, because you will get 30 or 40 more at least. If you lay off 200 and 40 more resign, then you have to quickly try to rehire from the layoff list.

After a layoff, a number of good positions will become available if you want to try for them. The company will need you more than ever before.

2. After a layoff, there is usually a shakeup in the high command. Top people resign, transfer, or depart to some other job. This opens up the channels for positions that normally would not be open for years, and, even then, would come one at a time. After a layoff, sometimes many higher positions are available immediately and simultaneously.

3. You may have put in many years with the company, and you don't want to lose your seniority or retirement benefits.

There are many other reasons you may want to remain. It may be a good place to work, you may have an interesting job and good friends in the workplace. Now that we have discussed why some want to survive the layoff, how can it be done? There are several ways:

1. Go on sick leave. When I decided to leave because a layoff was near, a co-worker told me that he was going to stay and ride it out. When he told his family doctor that he

was tired, nervous, and overworked, the doctor prescribed a long rest and gave my friend a letter to that effect.

My colleague received his pay for three months, survived the layoff, and returned to a higher position than he had before he left.

2. Ask for an immediate leave of absence without pay for personal reasons. Get another job if you need the income. Later when things settle down, you can return in the same way as my "sick" friend did.

3. Go as high as you can in the company to ask for a personal interview. Explain your personal situation, the reasons you want to stay, and what *mutual* benefits will accrue. Be sure that you go high enough so that the person is not likely to be laid off too. Such a sponsor, who agrees with your ideas or plans, can keep you on.

4. If the company is big enough and has branch offices in other parts of the country, consider requesting a transfer to another city, state, or even overseas. If a person really wants to remain with the company for seniority or pension rights, this may be the only way left.

Although a layoff disrupts many careers, if you keep your head and don't panic, it can, in the long run, be of benefit to you. However, more people get hurt than benefit in a layoff. As with a terrible natural disaster, it is better if you can avoid it by moving rather than sitting tight and riding out the storm.

16
Logbooks

As someday it may happen that a victim must be found,
I've got a little list—I've got a little list.
—*Gilbert & Sullivan*, The Mikado

As a student, I was taught to keep a logbook in which to enter the major events of the day. Once you acquire the habit, it takes no time at all. Usually, five or ten minutes at the end of each business day is all that is required. Over the years I continued this habit of keeping my daily log, in which I enter whatever I believe is worth noting.

I strongly urge that you start and maintain a logbook. Some entries can help your career and some can help defend you later in situations that might harm your career. Following are some of the advantages:

1. A logbook, over the long run, is your own evaluation of your progress. You can read it every month or so and decide if you are getting anywhere on your long-range career plan or not.

2. It is a good place to record items or directions you were given verbally that later may be forgotten or misinterpreted.

3. When others know you keep a log of what you do every day, and why, they are likely to give you more explicit and clear instructions.

4. A logbook is a handy reference if you have to write a report to explain events that developed over a long period of time.

5. It is invaluable if, for any reason, some serious or legal question develops as to who thought up an idea over which a patent rights fight later ensues, or whose idea it was that resulted in a breakthrough. I have been advised that in some situations a well-kept logbook has been used in courts of law when there were no other documents available. This is especially true when the matter is too complex for anyone to recreate from memory alone or if one testimony contradicts another. A logbook makes testimony much more believable.

Following are several examples in which my logbook was of great help:

1. I went to my boss to request a raise for a deserving woman who worked in our computer department. He listened and approved. I assumed that he would take care of her raise, but he forgot all about it.

Several months later, with no raise showing in her paycheck, the woman asked me about it. My boss said he didn't remember it at all, but he would do it right away. I asked him about the loss of three months' back pay and the loss of time in grade for her next promotion. Since he had no recollection of discussing it before, the boss said he could not justify a retroactive promotion. I read him my logbook entry which mentioned that he had cut our meeting short because he was going on a business trip. Then he remembered, and the woman got her retroactive raise. The boss also apologized to her.

2. We were working on a long-term research project for a client who had to take a two-month trip to Europe. During her absence, she turned over the direction of the research project to a subordinate.

A year or so after the project had been completed, I was called to the original manager's office. She was visibly upset and asked me why we had changed direction in the middle of the completed research project.

From my logbook I was able to recreate a step-by-step series of events, in chronological order, with dates of conferences and who said what to whom. That record made clear that we had followed the subordinate's directions while the manager was in Europe. She thanked me and said it was helpful to her because her superiors were asking her why certain changes were made. She didn't know and her subordinate didn't remember.

3. Countless times during my career, clients or superiors gave me verbal orders which I always wrote in my logbook. Many times, later on, I would be asked why I did a particular thing (especially when it didn't work out). If I said I followed orders, the boss would deny or not remember telling me that. However, showing him the entry and the date in my logbook prevented further argument or denial.

4. One client, at the end of a job, was upset that an overrun had occurred. We explained it was caused by changes in the project that were given to us by the client's technical director. We had been told to take his direction on all technical matters.

My logbook listed the dates and costs for the changes. The client's technical director agreed that he had given us verbal orders to make each change, but he hadn't figured the costs in advance or kept track of changes. We were paid, but the experience taught me thereafter to get each change priced each time we received one and to submit it to the client for approval.

I have been with my current company for 16 years, and if you ask me what I did on any given working day and why, I can tell you in a few minutes from my logbook. I store the logbooks as I fill them up and keep them in case they are ever needed for future reference.

It is part of my daily routine to make a brief entry just before I go home each evening. Often, someone will ask if

I can recall the date some client visited, so he can write a letter and refer to the visit. The logbook is also a record of when someone reported for work, was transferred, or resigned.

It is to your advantage to start and maintain a logbook if you have not already done so, and keep it up to date. You never know when such a simple thing can be of tremendous help to you in your career.

17
Loyalty

I don't want a brilliant staff! I want a loyal one.
—General George Patton

A recent survey of senior executives and managers revealed that the characteristic they prize most highly in their subordinates is loyalty.

Consider the situation in which the boss calls together a group of senior managers to plan some future course of action or some business investment. Several plans and ideas are submitted, discussed, and modified; finally it's up to the boss to choose one. Whatever the boss decides upon should receive everyone's loyal support, even if one disagrees with the plan from a business, technical, or financial point of view.

Naturally, you owe your boss your honest opinion if you believe that he or she is about to make a mistake, but remember the boss is the decision maker. If you cannot support the decision, then honestly say so at the start, so the boss won't depend on you to help implement the plan.

Sometimes our egos get in the way of our better judgment. We hurt our company, our peers, superiors, and subordinates just to prove we were right. It is difficult for someone to loyally work hard and long on a project about which he or she has doubts. Most bosses know their people well enough to know whom they can rely upon. These are the people a boss will hang onto at all costs. Napoleon once said, "Success has a thousand fathers, but defeat is an orphan." It's easy to support a winner. Sticking with the boss when the issue is in doubt is the real test of loyalty.

When you take a job, if you can't support or believe in the company, it's goals, or its method of operation, you would be wise to leave. If you find it impossible to support your boss's goals or methods, you should seek a transfer or other employment.

Loyalty isn't always doing whatever you are told in blind obedience. It's being open with your bosses, peers, and clients. If you honestly advise them in advance that you cannot support the plan, they will reassign the project to someone else.

The rewards of loyalty are rapid career advancement in one's chosen field and recognition from others that you can be relied upon to support whatever you are working on. Once embarked on the job, if you can be relied upon to see a project all the way through, you become a valuable asset to your superiors. The essence of good management is selecting and retaining good people who place loyalty at the top of the list. It's a rare and valuable asset.

18
Mid-Career Crisis

In the typical British tradition, he concluded that the
problem was behind him, because it had not arrived yet.
—*Winston S. Churchill*

This chapter discusses what has been called the mid-career
crisis that seems to affect career men and women somewhere around the age of 40, although it may occur at a
variety of ages. So let's define mid-career as occurring
somewhere between 35 and 50, give or take a few years.

Persons in mid-career take stock of their careers and
find them to be less than satisfying. There is a yearning for
something better and these people may or may not know
what it is that they want from a career. They only know
they don't want what they have and they want a change.

Another reason can be that the person concerned has
been working successfully at a job for purely financial reasons. He has a home and family to support and works
successfully at the job, but suddenly the youngest child is
out of college. The house is empty. He and his wife find
they no longer need the big house, children don't need
teeth straightened, school expenses are over, and he wants
a new career that pays and demands less. The fear of a
fresh start in a new venture can create a mid-career crisis.
This crisis can be intensified if one of the marriage part-
ners wants the change and the other does not.

A third, and probably most brutal, mid-career crisis occurs when a man or woman is suddenly fired or dismissed from a fairly high position in an organization.

Company mergers often result in a number of high-level dismissals. Changes in technology can put a senior man or woman out of date and then suddenly out of a job. Internal company politics can result in the sudden forced resignation of a manager or executive. A sudden change in a business environment (a stock market slump) can leave highly paid people out of work.

It is the third category of mid-career crisis this chapter will address. The first two vary on an almost individual basis and often require professional (psychological or clerical) advice.

In the third type of mid-career crisis I have observed the patterns of behavior of those who have handled it fairly well and those who have not. Let's consider several examples.

A Ph.D. who was a college professor of mathematics left the university in pursuit of higher salary and more rapid career advancement. He joined a research and development think tank. Several years later he was released along with 400 or so others in a general reduction of staff. He was so hurt by the dismissal he went home and stayed in the house—ashamed of himself. His wife, a former school teacher, had to return to work, first on a part-time and later a full-time basis to support the family.

Four years later he is still minding the house and getting the children off to school while his wife is the breadwinner. I don't know if this man ever intends to return to the labor market. I do know, however, that the longer he waits (four years is already too long), the more difficult it will be for him to explain his years at home.

A senior engineer was released with three months' severance pay. He went home and became hyperactive on home improvement projects. He bought several hand power tools and began to fix doors, repaint the house, and, in general, do all those projects that one never seems to have time for when employed. He also raised a vegetable garden.

He never seemed to find time to go look for another job. He told me that he had saved several thousand dollars on his home improvement projects. What he was doing was much akin to the wife who "saved" her husband $2,000 by buying a $4,000 mink coat that was on sale for $2,000.

Finally, when financial need forced him out of the house, he found another job. He did it when he had to do it, but not before.

Another senior engineer who lost his job didn't let his ego bother him. He called everyone he could think of, including me, to explain what had happened and to ask assistance in finding a new job. Of course, we all pitched in and started looking around for him.

A week or so later he called me to announce he had a new job even better than his old one. He got in in an odd manner. His wife, at a weekly bridge gathering, told her friends about her husband's situation. One of the bridge players was the wife of an executive in an electronics company. She told her husband, who called the unemployed engineer and offered him the new and better job.

A man in his early forties was caught in the 1970 recession. He was given three months notice, and he took it well. His date of departure was June 30.

I remember coming into work after the July Fourth holiday and seeing this fellow going into his office, carrying his briefcase. Several days later I saw him again coming into work. Then I asked his manager why this fellow was coming into work since his pay had stopped on June 30. His answer surprised me. I was told that he just kept coming into work. He sat at his desk all day and went home in the evening.

I asked the manager to have the man come in to see me. When he came, I asked if he had another job. He said no. I asked if he had looked for another job; he said no. I asked why he kept coming into work after June 30, and he said he didn't know what else to do. He was embarrassed that his neighbors might observe him staying at home, so he came to work. Also, he said his wife wanted him out of the house.

Fortunately, a few phone calls produced several appointments at other companies. Later, I heard he accepted one of the positions. (The person who hired him called us; the fellow who got the job didn't call. I guess he was too embarrassed.)

It had never occurred to us that a man of his age, with his professional background and education and three months' time to find another job, would react that way and do nothing. I hope he never is in that situation again because he probably couldn't handle it.

Here you see four different reactions to an almost identical mid-career crisis. From my own observations let me list some things that I think you shouldn't do and some things I think you should do in such a situation.

1. Don't panic. It isn't the end of the world.

2. Don't withdraw for a long period of contemplation, even if you have money in the bank. That will disappear rapidly if you maintain your former standard of living.

3. Don't rush to take the first job you can get. That is usually a mistake, and a second move soon follows. Everyone understands one mid-career crisis, but two or three indicate something may be wrong with you.

4. Don't wait until you are unemployed to look for another job. You may have been working for 20 years for

the same company, and it may give you three or six months' notice. Use it. Don't think that something will come up before you have to leave. What if it doesn't?

5. When you go out on interviews, don't cry or complain about how badly you were treated by your former employer. That will only hurt you.

6. Use your contacts and friends. Most will be glad to help. Maybe they will need the same from you someday. Even the most hard-driving executive turns a kind ear in response to this type of request for assistance.

7. Don't refuse to consider a position at a lower salary than your former job. It's better to have a job at $25,000 a year than to be out of a job that formerly paid $50,000 a year.

8. Don't lie to cover the reason you are looking for a new job. If you were laid off, say so. It's no disgrace, especially so when the reasons were not your fault (merger or economic conditions).

9. Don't pretend that you really don't need the job. Most of us work out of necessity, so don't be afraid to admit it.

A few things to consider doing when you suddenly lose your job in mid-career are:

1. Take a long and careful look at yourself and your situation. This is a time to use your intelligence, so think about it well. How did it happen? What should you do? How? Who can help? Should you consider changing careers? If so, to what?

2. The older you are, the more difficult it will be for you to find a new position of equal or higher status. Some of the reasons are that automatic salary increases may have put your salary out of range and years with the same company may result in your job knowledge and experience being related primarily to one company, and these may not be transferable. This is more true in administrative or

legal positions than in technical or accounting positions because these special talents are transferable more easily from one place to another.

3. Your experience has some value and is marketable if properly sold to a new organization.

4. Try to be adaptable and open to new ideas and change. One of the reasons that companies shy away from older people is the fear that they become fixed and rigid in their ways of working as they become older. Unfortunately, this is often true. Don't you be like that.

5. Move with deliberate, planned speed. Prepare your résumé well. Select several places; don't mail résumés all over the place. Prepare a personal, typed cover letter to accompany your résumé. Prepare your résumé to match the place to which you apply. Emphasize that part of your experience that pertains to the job you are seeking.

6. Direct your résumé and letter to a person. Writing an unsolicited résumé to the personnel department generally gets you nowhere.

7. Try to make your contact as high as possible. If you send your résumé to a general manager who passes it down for action into the organization, you can be sure you will get a reply and possibly an interview with a branch chief.

When you meet the branch chief, mention that you know the general manager, if you do. If you don't know the manager, don't mention it; the branch chief may assume that you do.

8. Try to carefully assess your assets and liabilities. When you select a place to apply, if you can't see how you can be of value there, then most surely an employer won't.

9. At the interview, be on time, sure of yourself, and positive. It is expected and understood that young people may be nervous at an interview, but "old pros" should not be nervous. Losing a good job can happen to anybody.

Now you start again with assurance, poise, and knowledge that you have much to give that is of value. If you don't exhibit this, then you put yourself at a disadvantage. Asking for help from strangers at an interview is also out of order. You don't need any help, just an opportunity to perform, and you will prove your worth.

10. If you have been between jobs for some months in trying to find a suitable position, say so. It is understandable that at mid-career it may take some time to find what you want. Up to a year is acceptable.

Don't say you were "consulting." Anyone who loses a job that pays less than $20,000 a year is unemployed, and those who lose jobs paying over $20,000 a year become "consultants." Don't say you consulted for 18 months unless you did and are prepared to give the names and addresses of your clients. This can be most embarrassing for you, but unfortunately, some people try this to account for a period of unemployment.

The mid-career crisis caused by sudden unemployment can produce severe problems. Statistics indicate that heart attacks, suicides, and divorces increase during periods of recession and unemployment. People reacting to the stress and depression caused by the loss of a job and status sometimes do strange things.

Like illness, injury, and accidents, the mid-career crisis can strike anyone. How an individual faces the problem and either masters it or is mastered by it will affect the remainder of a person's life. Some start new careers and later bless the day that they were laid off, because it forced them to do what they should have done years earlier. Many became very successful. I have seen others collapse, get divorced, and never recover. It's all up to the individual.

19
Mistakes

The man who makes no mistakes does not usually make anything. —*Edward J. Phelps*

Experience is the name everyone gives to their mistakes. —*Oscar Wilde*

To make a mistake is "to understand or perceive wrongly" or "to interpret or judge incorrectly."

We all make mistakes. The best one can say for mistakes is that one can learn from them. When we do something correctly, we know just what to do, and we do it well. This may be satisfying to our egos, but we really didn't learn anything new.

Mistakes, however, are a different matter. To benefit from them we must view them in their proper perspective. If we don't study and review our mistakes, then we will repeat them.

In accidents, the initial bump may cause little damage, but the secondary crash that follows is the killer. Similarly, the initial mistake may not be too bad, but the follow-up actions to correct or hide the error may become the serious mistakes that do permanent damage. For example, consider a social situation in which someone inadvertently commits a faux pas and offends some friend. The initial mistake has occurred. It's what comes next that either solves the problem or causes permanent damage. If an

121

apology is given and accepted, the damage is repaired, and the problem is forgotten.

Often, however, a person ignores the simple solution of a sincere apology. The offending party's ego compels him to make little of what happened and to make the offended party appear as a poor sport or too sensitive. In effect, the wrongdoer blames the victim for the mistake. Such behavior is the secondary mistake that causes more damage than the original one. In this situation the usual result is a lost friend.

When we try to hide or lie about a mistake at work, the secondary mistakes are generally far worse than the first and do severe and permanent damage to all concerned. It is better to be known for making honest mistakes than to be known as someone whose word cannot be relied upon. We all make mistakes; it's how we handle them that matters.

The way some people try to avoid mistakes is to avoid making decisions or taking action, because decision and action have potential for errors. A common complaint from higher management is that people won't make decisions. They are afraid of being wrong or making a mistake. They don't understand that they are making the biggest mistake of their lives. Indecision or inaction seems to be so ingrained in one's personality that it appears almost impossible to change. For these people, it's easier to let someone else do it and then let others point out, after the fact, what should have been done.

Let us discuss those who do things and make their share of mistakes. How do they handle their mistakes? What do they do about them? A great deal depends upon how the individuals look upon those mistakes. Usually, the first person who realizes he or she has made a mistake is the person who did it.

The person who does not admit to any mistakes has

arrived at step one in what we will call the "error process." If you won't admit to making the mistake in the first place, then you'll never benefit from the costly lesson that errors can teach us. You paid the tuition, but you stopped going to class. The person who stops here will be a repeater. Little can be done with such people. They won't let anyone help them.

Some people realize they have made a mistake and accept the fact. Are they willing to discuss it openly with others and accept comments or criticism? If not, they are at level two of our "error process" and stop short in the learning process.

Let us now move on to level three of our "error process" or into the learning stage. We benefit from the mistake if we learn how to correct it and how to prevent doing it again. It's worth the effort to get to level three. By asking for help, or by freely discussing our mistake, we can receive information and assistance from others. Discuss what has occurred, so you can see for yourself what you should do the next time, or what not to do again.

Most managers deeply appreciate being advised by subordinates when an error has occurred. Managers usually are most understanding when you tell them about it. When they discover it for themselves, or, worse, when some superior or customer tells them, then that's another story. Then the boss seeks you out, and if he finds you hung up at level one or two of our "error process," you deserve whatever happens next. If you are unable to approach your boss because the reaction is too violent or emotional when you explain what went wrong, the solution is to get another boss. You won't go far in that job or in those circumstances.

Don't make the same mistake twice. Be creative and always make new mistakes, so you can be ever learning something new. The problem is that most people tend to be repeaters. They never seem to learn and as a result bury their careers either intentionally or in all innocence.

Wherever we work we find our share of chronic latecomers. This is a bad habit those people do not choose to change. We also have the clock watchers. This, too, is a bad habit those so afflicted won't change. We have the "doers" and the "lookers on." Again, we see work habits that some find too ingrained to change. These people are hung up at level one of our "error process." They can't be helped, because they won't be helped.

There are some who refuse help when it is offered. Some gladly discuss your errors and mistakes, past and present, with you or anyone else, but they won't discuss their own. There are chronic complainers and critics. These people are hung up at level two of our "error process." These, also, are difficult to help, because they know they make mistakes, but won't let anyone discuss it, so they become repeaters.

In the remaining group, those at level three are usually successful people. They seem to rise to the higher levels wherever they work. They make mistakes, but you don't find them repeating the same mistakes. They learn and grow.

The more things we do, the more mistakes we will make. It is what we do afterward that counts.

20
Obedience

Wouldst thou prove thy constancy, prove first thy
obedience.   —*John Milton*

Obedience means carrying out a command, submitting to
control, or responding to duty. It is not easy to be obedient. In today's "do your own thing" world, it is not considered desirable to be obedient or in any way accom-
modating unless you fully agree with what is going on at all
times. Obedient people today may be looked down upon
as lacking in initiative, drive, or ability.

I have asked some priests and nuns, who have taken
vows of poverty, chastity, and obedience, which vow is the
most difficult to observe. I have asked career military personnel, who swear oaths of obedience to higher lawful
authority, what is the hardest part of working in a military
career. In all cases, I was told that obedience is the most
difficult. Little wonder then that the rest of us, who don't
take any vows of obedience, find it difficult to obey lawful
orders or legitimate directions given from those above us
at work or school, especially when we don't like the order
or disagree with some part or all of it.

This chapter is not discussing blind obedience, in which
one follows all orders without consideration of the moral
or ethical aspect of the order. No one should do anything
that is against one's personal code of ethics, illegal, or unfair and then later try to justify it by claiming obedience to
higher authority. The scope of this chapter is restricted to

obedience of authority on nonmoral and nonlegal issues, or the routine, everyday matters that come up at work and elsewhere.

At work or school there are usually clearly defined lines of authority. At work, everyone has a boss and rules to follow or a goal to reach. At school, everyone has a teacher, principal, or dean who is in authority, subjects to study and learn, and tests to pass. The question is how we relate to figures of authority. Most people agree that these figures have legitimate authority and that we should obey such authority within the confines of our work or school.

Yet, do we find it so in our everyday activities? We find little or no difficulty in obeying an order or request with which we agree. We cheerfully and willingly do it as long as we agree and understand what it's all about.

Obedience becomes difficult when you are asked or directed to do some job you don't like to do, or in a manner that you think is incorrect. Under such circumstances, many people, consciously or subconsciously, overtly or covertly, try to disobey, delay, or obfuscate. They may even get angry and create problems with others. They can be very creative in thinking up reasons for not obeying. Some classic excuses and tactics are to be too busy to get around to it, to "forget," to wait to see if you really meant it, to talk it over again, to avoid contact and communication and hope it all blows over, to ignore it in hopes it will go away in time, and to postpone or delay action.

As a manager, you must be on the alert for this type of behavior, because it can, at times, be most disruptive. Two examples follow:

Upon being advised that he must dismiss a chronic troublemaker in his section, one of our managers told me that he didn't want to be the one to do it. I reminded the manager that it was his job and his responsibility to let the employee go. He had been warned repeatedly, given written notice to improve, but continued to disregard his manager and create problems.

Several weeks later, I saw the employee still at work. When I asked his manager about it, he said he had been so busy and didn't have time to dismiss the fellow concerned.

This was a case of disobedience, because the manager did not want to carry out this unpleasant, but necessary, task. He delayed and tried other ploys, as best he could, to have someone else (anyone else) do the dirty work for him.

In another instance, a disagreement arose over what kind of company party or picnic to have for employees during the summer. A committee was to recommend three alternatives to the boss as a suitable company-paid event. The boss chose the third alternative and advised the committee to get the tickets and make the arrangements. As the time for the company picnic approached, the boss realized that he had heard nothing further from the committee, so he called them in and asked why. The boss learned that two of the three members of the committee disliked the alternative he had chosen, so they quietly stopped work on the project. The third member did nothing because the other two had quit working on the affair. There was no company picnic that year.

No good manager wants total, unquestioning obedience. What the manager expects and has a right to receive are honest, open opinions and options. When the manager decides, he should be able to expect that the staff will support the decision or plan and try to make it work.

Most managers respect those who are not afraid to express dissenting opinions if they are well thought out and not made in an emotional manner. If the manager sees one who disagreed with the decision work hard to make it succeed, he realizes how difficult this can be for anyone and appreciates the effort.

There are certain steps managers or supervisors can

take when they think someone is not in full agreement with a plan of action so as to reduce the risk of disobedience or delay. Managers can:

1. Write the order or plan.
2. Define, in writing, exactly what is expected from the person concerned.
3. Leave no alternatives or options available.
4. Write a time by which this task should be completed.
5. Request written acknowledgment from the recipient.
6. React quickly to any delay, or uncooperative attitudes, and take corrective action.

Some people have a tendency to "test the water" when they don't agree with a plan to see if you will do anything about their disobedience. Others will silently watch the contest. If you don't get it done the way you want, then others will soon follow suit and you will find even your most simple and routine orders will be questioned or ignored. You won't remain a manager long if you let such a situation develop and persist. When superiors have to correct such a situation, usually the manager is replaced.

If you honestly believe you can't fully cooperate, then you should clearly say so and ask to be relieved from the task or project before it starts. Don't take the assignment and then "drag your feet," or keep trying to "correct" it. Of course, if we all refused to cooperate unless we fully agreed with everything all of the time, then nothing would ever get done.

Those who do their best regardless of personal feelings go further in their chosen profession. There's nothing wrong with obeying legitimate authority if you disagree, as long as no moral, legal, or ethical issues are concerned.

This is not to be construed as advising anyone to never

insist upon doing the job his or her own way. On the contrary, when it is your responsibility to make the decision or the choice, do so, and do it the way you think best. It is when you are subordinate to the decision maker that you should either make your objections known at the start, or else obey the lawful authority of the manager.

21
Office Romance

When I behold upon the night's starr'd face, huge cloudy symbols of a high romance.   —*John Keats*

What have business and romance got to do with each other? Theoretically nothing, but in practice, possibly a great deal. Because this book is intended for the person who wants to advance his or her career, this topic is included for several reasons:

1. An office romance can adversely affect your career even if you are an innocent bystander in no way involved.

2. It is not wise to become romantically involved at work even if it is legitimate (both parties single at the time).

3. An illicit or extramarital affair between persons in the same workplace will eventually become known, no matter how careful or clever participants think they are.

As you gain some work experience, sooner or later you will encounter this difficult situation, and if you get involved or handle it badly, it can adversely affect your career. A senior executive who doesn't want anyone at work, wife, or family to find out about his involvement in an office romance can be dangerous to the job security of others. You may be the best person in his group, but if he thinks you can be a threat to him in any way, he will move against you and make you pay the price of his indiscretions.

My secretary once mentioned an office romance to me

when she knew I was going to have business contact with one of the parties, to put me on my guard so I wouldn't commit a faux pas and put myself in an embarrassing situation. Secretaries seem to know what is going on before the bosses know.

Let's assume that you are not involved in one, but others with whom you work are. What do you do? Here are some recommendations that time and experience have shown to be helpful:

First, if your boss is in any way involved, then "hear no evil, see no evil, speak no evil." People strike hard and violently when a subordinate is of danger to them in this situation. They have far more than a job to protect, so they will get rid of you fast. They can't fire you officially because you found out they were "running around." They would never put that on your record as a reason for dismissing you, but they can find a "valid" reason, and you will be the loser in the long run. So stay away from this situation. Don't even talk about it at home. This can be even worse if your family knows the boss's family socially or even casually.

The next situation is when the romance involves subordinates for whom you are responsible. Then, you have to get involved whether you like it or not. You can rationalize your inactivity by saying it is none of your business what other people do after hours on their own time. You have to face the fact that sooner or later it will affect office efficiency and morale, and that is your responsibility. An office romance can result in an unjustified promotion or merit raise bestowed on one involved party by the other party. You can also expect the opposite when they break up.

The best action is preventive medicine. Let it be clearly known and understood, in advance, that you manage a place of business; explain what will happen if you ever learn of such a situation going on, and make no exceptions.

How do you know it is going on? There are a number of signs.

1. Unjustified raises or recommendations that don't seem reasonable to you.

2. Chronic late arrivals to work or early departures with no action taken by the supervisor who is usually strict about such things when it involves others.

3. Some one or two people suddenly turning against each other for no outwardly apparent business reason.

4. Coincidental absences from work (sick leave, days off, or part of a day off at the same time).

5. Requests for assignments with specific people for no apparent business reason.

6. Requests for transfers or reassignments for no apparent business reason.

7. People talking to each other too much in the corner of the office (alone).

8. People not talking to each other at a business meeting or on the job when they should.

There can be other perfectly valid reasons for the actions listed, but if several show up, you had better look into it. Watch to see if other signs reveal themselves. Ask your secretary. Sometimes this inquiry in itself has been known to stop it. She passes the word down the "grapevine" that the boss was asking about the situation. Remember, the "grapevine" works both ways.

If an office romance becomes an obvious problem, affecting office efficiency and disrupting routine, a manager must deal with it diplomatically. You let them know that you know by not saying that you know. They must conclude that you know. A good diplomat can make a point known without ever saying it directly. The only justification you, as the manager, can have for bringing the subject up is your concern for office efficiency, morale, or production. Make this point clear to those involved. You are not approving or disapproving personal behavior. You are concerned only with how such behavior affects your area of responsibility at work.

Some of my friends and business associates have chosen to ignore such situations. As managers of one or both of the participants, they became involved later when an irate husband, wife, or mother showed up at the personnel office.

When a mother showed up, one of my friends told me this story. He had a junior manager in his group who was about 35 years old and married with young children. The junior manager had a small group of five or six people, and he hired only women (this first clue the boss had over-looked). One of the women was a young single girl, and the junior manager was taking her off weekends to go skiing together.

When her mother found out, she appeared at the company office demanding to see the general manager. My friend, who was a senior manager, was called on the carpet because it involved someone in his department, even though he didn't know what was going on. In retrospect, he said he should have been alert to what was happening (the junior manager had a "harem" and went from one to the other) since the junior manager hired only women for his group.

Such situations have nothing to do with your professional ability or talent in handling complex jobs, but such things can hurt you personally or damage your career. Keep a weather eye out so you are not suddenly called in one day to a boss's office where the head of personnel and perhaps a company lawyer hold you accountable. Ignorance is no excuse here, and if you admit you knew about it and did nothing, that's even worse.

It goes without saying, of course, that you clear all such activity beforehand with your immediate supervisor and get his or her approval or permission. In doing this before the fact and getting your policies on such matters cleared up in advance, it's much easier to act if and when you see a situation developing.

If your superior approves, then you are free to act as you think best. If your superior tells you to keep hands off, then, of course, do so, but advise him or her if and when you see a problem developing. Then step aside just as you were told to do. If you keep a daily logbook, listing the events of the day, write that you were told to ignore such situations or take no action. It may be your salvation later on.

If you change bosses, go see the new one, get another understanding on this subject, and act accordingly. This may be the only defense you will have later on.

22
Personalities

"My idea of an agreeable person," said Hugo Bohun, "is someone who agrees with me." —*Benjamin Disraeli*

The mark of the successful executive reverberates throughout the company in which he operates. He gets things done; things hum along efficiently under his overall direction and guidance; sales increase; efficiency rises; morale soars; and profits climb. The company grows, more personnel are hired, and the employees, the management, and the stockholders are happy.

One of the most important acts of any executive is the selection of personnel for a variety of jobs and changing situations. The ability to pick the right person for the right job can work wonders. Failure to do so upsets just about everything.

Most of us have read or heard about the Peter Principle. People rise to their level of incompetence and spend the rest of their lives in misery trying to work one level "over their heads" in a job they can't do well.

We all have seen the top salesman get promoted to manager and then fall flat on his face. We have seen the production worker become a foreman and get fired for nonperformance. We have witnessed the senior staff analyst who fails miserably when he takes over a line-management position.

In sports, many top athletes fail as managers or coaches. Most successful managers and coaches were by no means the best athletes in their playing days; the opposite seems to be true.

The reason for such failures is that someone put the wrong man in the wrong job. Why? Certainly not on purpose. It should be clear that the talents for coaching are not the same as for playing. The abilities required for management are not the same as those required of a top production worker, salesperson, or engineer.

It seems that the reward for success or excellence in your chosen field is to be rapidly promoted out of it into some area where you know little and can only grope along. Why does this happen? Perhaps senior people believe that good men can adapt to and learn any job. This is just not so. People work for many different reasons. They respond to different stimuli, and sometimes an individual "hears a different drummer."

When you appoint a new person to a new job, you take a chance and, as in marriage, you find out what it's like only afterward. Can you do anything in advance to reduce the uncertainty and risk of failure? There is something that can be done if you are willing to take the time and trouble to lay it all out and study the problem ahead of time, piece by piece.

What follows here is by no means infallible or all-inclusive, but it can be used effectively in conjunction with other pertinent information any good executive can gather to aid in making decisions about who to put where.

There are different types of work, and there are different types of people. Can we somehow match them up in a sensible manner that reduces the risk of failure?

The different types of work can be classified in terms of the personal qualifications needed to do the job.

1. *Operating work* is usually repetitive and requires doing rather than planning. It demands a relatively lower degree of imagination and analytical capability.

2. *Analytical work,* such as staff studies performed by scientists and engineers or financial studies and analyses require highly developed problem-solving skills and analytical ability.

3. *Technical work* involves knowledge of a specialized field, such as mathematics, computer programming, chemistry, or accounting. This knowledge is gained through prior education and on-the-job experience.

4. *Creative work,* such as scientific research, advertising, and writing, requires a high degree of imagination and vision and the ability to germinate original ideas.

5. *Administrative work* from top management down to the first-line foreman requires ability to exercise authority and capacity to direct and get things done through others. You do not do the job yourself.

6. *Leadership* such as that of the president and/or top manager or director must inspire all others to effective performance.

Even at low levels, the jobs can combine two or more basic types of work, but one usually predominates. The higher the position, the more varied the types of work will become.

A highly creative person usually dislikes routine, and, if routine tasks are forced on him, he won't do them well and his skills will be wasted. A person who is good at the operating level and enjoys working with details, routine, and repetitive assignments will not necessarily be a good analyst, administrator, or leader.

Thus, positions requiring several different types of work demand versatility from the individual. The number of qualifiied personnel decreases rapidly as the range of work assigned to a position increases.

Like the mother who doesn't train her 10-year-old daughter in cooking or helping in the kitchen, because the mother can do the job faster, the company that does not try to screen personnel before hiring them or train them on the job will pay the price later in bad performance, resentment, and a high probability of eventual failure for all concerned.

At this stage, we have tried to codify the various types of positions. Now, let us try to identify the various types of people and then try to match them with each other.

In the August 1971 issue of *Executive Digest*, on page one, an article about how to get along with people said that behavioral scientists classified everyone into one of four general personality categories. Each one, they said, lives in a different world of thought, emotion, sensation, and time. Let us list the four different types as behavioral scientists define them.

1. The *sensation type* lives in the present, with little interest in the past or future. Because his energies are so directed, he tends to be most effective in coping with immediate situations. He is a doer, not a planner, believes in action now, and is impatient of delays for any reason.

2. The *intuitive type* sees the future as more real than either the past or present. He is a planner, is highly intuitive, is subject to subsconscious promptings, and has a capacity for intuitive thinking. He often appears to be flighty, impractical, and unrealistic. His behavior is often conditioned, not by what is happening, but by what he believes is going to happen. He pays little attention to time.

3. The *feeling type* is most effective in the area of emotions. The past is important to him and he tends to judge the present by the past and new friends by old ones. New situations make him uncomfortable unless he can relate them with some past occurrence with which he has dealt before. It's easy for him to lose track of time.

4. The *thinking type* takes a logical view of the world. He is long on planning and patience and he lives by the clock.

He is at his worst when circumstances demand that he "play it by ear" or when plans go awry.

Each of us falls into one of these four types, although we may overlap in that we have tendencies or desires that fall into more than one category. If this is so, there is still one of the four areas in which our personality predominates, so let us try to find the type of position that fits our strongest desires or interests.

By now you can probably see what is coming next. I will create a table or matrix in which we can try to fit the man or woman by personality type to the various types of jobs previously described.

None of this will work, of course, unless it is assumed that you know the person who is going to be promoted or assigned to the new job. This is done by careful, periodic review of each employee's performance, say every six months or so, and the record is kept in personnel files. It is amazing how accurate a picture one can get of an individual by reading, at one time, several well-written personnel evaluation reports of his performance over an extended period of time.

If the employee is a new hire, then he should be carefully screened and checked out before being placed in areas of authority or responsibility for his first assignment in your company. Past references mean little, because all bosses tend to be too kind in their letters of recommendation, they don't really care any more how well the person does, and the old boss is not responsible any more. I have read many excellent recommendations that currently unemployed scientists and engineers are carrying around with them. If they were half as good as the letters say, they should never have been released from employment.

Also, the opposite can be true. A good man could have

been released by an incompetent supervisor who was afraid of the competition from a highly qualified subordinate. This type of supervisor will unnecessarily downgrade the applicant to justify his own erroneous decision to release him.

So you must be careful in using references from outside your own organization in judging anyone. It is best to investigate, test, study, and decide for yourself in choosing employees.

But let us get back to what I will call our "capabilities index." We attempt in this table to match various personality types to various job types. The final decision, of course, is left to the executive given the responsibility to select or assign personnel in his group to the tasks under his authority.

CAPABILITIES INDEX TABLE

Job Classification	Personality Type			
	Sensation	*Intuitive*	*Feeling*	*Thinking*
Operating	Yes	No	No	Yes
Analytical	No	No	No	Yes
Technical	No	No	Yes	Yes
Creative	No	Yes	Yes	No
Administrative	Yes	No	Yes	No
Top Leadership	No	Yes	No	No

This table is only an attempt to systematize the person and the job and aid the executive in matching them. It has worked fairly well for us, and I hope it will for you as well.

23
The Peter Principle

He didn't know what to do, so he did what he knew.
—Old Army saying

It is an unfortunate but too true fact of life that all of us are not cut out or suited for top positions in our chosen careers. For one reason or another, few ever will reach the top, no matter where we work and how hard we try.

Among many reasons for this, few top jobs are available. The demands made on a person to reach the top require ability, dedication, drive, and initiative that few of us possess to the required degree. The reasons are too numerous and complex for anyone to list, but a basic fact may be that the job is simply beyond the abilities of the person seeking the position, or worse, beyond the abilities of the person currently holding the job.

The Peter Principle refers to the tendency of people to rise to their level of incompetence and then spend the rest of their careers unhappily trying without success to do a job they cannot do well.

Sad examples of this are the outstanding professor who is elevated to head of a department because she is an excellent scholar, researcher, or teacher, but fails as department head because of inability to handle a budget; or the top salesman who is promoted to sales manager but can't handle the job because he can't direct others to do what he did well.

The results of having the wrong person in the wrong job

can be disastrous and, as with most disasters, warning signals are emitted that indicate worse events to come.

Most major earthquakes give off early warning in small tremors that can be detected, if the personnel responsible are alert to detect these signs. The recent oil shortage did not come upon us unannounced. Signs were present several years earlier. We just ignored them.

In human behavior, in some situations, people give off certain signs that indicate trouble ahead. These can be sensed and noted if the people with whom they come in contact are alert and sensitive enough to receive these signals and know what they mean and so can take action in time.

Personnel who are working in positions for which they are not qualified also emit early warning signals by behavior that indicates all is not well. It is the job of supervisors in any organization to note these signs and, if possible, take corrective action before a major crisis occurs.

It is usually the personnel one level below the person in trouble who first note the early signs of problems to come, but they are reluctant to say or do anything because the problem person is their boss. They are afraid that if they bring this to the attention of higher management they will suffer.

A subordinate is placed in a difficult position by an incompetent superior in the organization. The fear of punishment plus loyalty for the boss results in inactivity and silence from those trapped by bad leadership.

In my experience, even when the people concerned were about to lose their jobs because of a manager's ineptness, they kept silent. The customer was at the point of canceling the contract because the work was going so badly. Upper management stepped in at the last minute, put things right, and saved the contract by replacing the manager.

When asked why they didn't speak up earlier when they

saw the difficulty and knew their jobs were in jeopardy, the subordinates said they didn't want to make trouble. This is a strange, but typical response in such situations. Senior personnel, therefore, must pick up the signals given off by a person who is not doing a job well.

Typical symptoms of people in over their heads are listed here, followed by a brief discussion of each one.

1. The "too busy" person shows activity but no action.
2. Attention to detail syndrome.
3. Don't know what to do.
4. Extreme sensitivity to criticism in any form.
5. Preoccupation with job perquisites.
6. Avoidance of blame.
7. Irritability and indecisiveness.

All these symptoms stem from one basic problem. The person involved knows either consciously or subconsciously that he is in a job he is unable to do well. Unable to cope with this situation, he tries to cover up the problem by a facade of jargon or behavior he thinks will indicate a mastery of the situation.

This list is not all-inclusive, but these seven symptoms are typical.

Symptom 1—Too busy. This may apply to the newly appointed or newly hired manager who wants to impress everyone with his energy and efficiency. He is not too sure yet what he really is supposed to do, but instead of taking time to study his job, ask questions, and find out what is required, he plunges headlong into a lot of useless activity. He overreacts and demonstrates great activity, but little action, and no results.

This symptom can be transient until the manager becomes more familiar and at ease with his new job. It should pass in several months' time. If not, then higher management should look again at the new appointee and possibly replace him before he does some real damage.

Another relatively harmless symptom of this stage is the obviously expensive attaché case that is carried everywhere, probably bulging with trivia. The new hires usually outgrow this stage. One rarely, if ever, sees veteran executives carrying such devices of importance. Having proved themselves by past performance, they need no external badges to impress anyone.

Symptom 2—Details. This symptom is an offshoot of the first, but it manifests itself in a different way. The inept or insecure manager shows his efficiency by bearing down hard on meaningless details. Everyone must be very prompt, and coffee must be ready precisely at 9:30 A.M.

These people act as if all small details were vitally important. They are unable to separate the important from the routine, so they spend much time and energy making the office look efficient. They upset people needlessly, compound existing problems, and provide no solutions.

They exhibit their insecurity for all to see. Unfortunately, some higher managers do not see through this symptom early enough to head off trouble. Such insecure persons are really telling everyone they need guidance and help. If they don't get it, the harm and hard feelings they cause will persist in the organization long after they depart.

Symptom 3—Don't know what to do. This problem arises when a manager is clearly over his head in his job. He doesn't really know what he should do, so he does things that he knows how to do even if they are the wrong things.

Let's say a person is appointed to head up a proposal team bidding on a new job. As proposal manager, he is in charge of all aspects of the job, technical, administrative, and financial. He has a weak technical but strong financial background, so he spends most of his time doing the accountant's job.

He did what he knew because he didn't know what to do as proposal manager. The results of this type of management are easily predictable. He delivers a neat, correctly priced proposal that is rejected as technically nonresponsive.

The opposite can occur when a technical-oriented manager does the job. He delivers the best technical proposal for far too much money and loses the bid on price. Both types lack proper judgment and the balance that is required of a manager.

Upper management had better move fast when it detects this symptom in a subordinate because he, too, is calling for help. I'm not sure if this problem is curable by more training or guidance. The person who shows this symptom may have reached one level above his ability to function efficiently, and demotion, reassignment, or termination may be the only answer.

Symptom 4—Too sensitive or insecure. If one finds that a new manager, after a recent promotion, has become sensitive to criticism, direct or implied, this may be a defense mechanism against his own incompetence. This sensitivity may cease if he adjusts well to his new position and gains poise and confidence.

The person who exhibits this symptom can do great harm to his organization because, among his other faults, this type fears subordinates who show superior skills or potential for rapid advancement. He may severely restrict these people from doing their jobs.

Incompetence breeds conscientious mediocrity. Such persons write countless memos on meaningless topics in an attempt to impress others.

Symptom 5—Job perquisites. It is understandable that when some people are promoted, they are so obviously pleased with the perquisites of the new position that they need some time to adjust.

For example, the young manager who suddenly is permitted to use the executive dining room may, at first, spend some extra time there, savoring his new surroundings and inviting unnecessary guests for lunch to impress them.

Reserved parking spaces, expense accounts, and other upper management perquisites require some time to use correctly and put in proper perspective.

If a person becomes obsessed with these management benefits instead of doing his job, this requires the attention of higher management. The person may be too immature for a leadership role.

Symptom 6—Avoiding blame. Any good manager is more than happy to pass on praise to those who deserve it. Also, he should be ready to take the blame for anything that goes wrong, because he must assume total job responsibility for the performance of each member of the group.

Some managers do the opposite. When things go well, the manager is first in line to take the credit. When things go wrong, he tries to assign the blame to others.

A manager who doesn't know the value of employee morale or the basic considerations of dealing with other human beings is not a good leader. When this symptom is spotted by higher management, rapid removal from the position is the best course. This symptom, once exhibited by a person, waxes and wanes, but never departs.

Symptom 7—Irritability and indecisiveness. Someone in a position where he is not performing well knows it first. If he is clever enough to conceal it from others for a time, this effort will take its toll.

A natural reaction to this pressure is to become irritable and easily upset, which is difficult to conceal. This symptom may be the first indicator to someone else that a person is having trouble with his new job.

Another indicator is indecisiveness. If the manager has trouble making decisions, constantly reverses himself, or makes general-type statements, he is not sure of himself or what he should do.

Many people find it difficult to communicate problems or uncertainties to others. Sometimes they don't face problems themselves. When this occurs, they send out distress signals as they try to cope with their own problems. Higher management must note these signs and take corrective action before others suffer needlessly.

24
Politics

Politics is perhaps the only profession for which no preparation is thought necessary.
—*Robert Louis Stevenson*

Office politics figures as a fact of life in any career. The higher you rise, the more it comes into play. You can, for a short period of time, choose to ignore it and refuse to participate, but that may be a big mistake.

The object of politics is to deal with people either to gain something that you want or to stop someone from doing something that can affect you or your interest disadvantageously. Of the two types of politics, offensive and defensive, the first is to get something, and the second is to stop someone from taking something from you.

By now, in your career, you realize that you are in a race or competition in this life. For whatever position you hold or aspire to, there are, very likely, others who want it. This is especially so as you rise to successively higher positions. Many people are just as qualified as you for the job, promotion, or transfer. Office politics is often the deciding factor in who gets the prize.

Let me present some examples:

In my second management position, at a large company, the chief engineer was a brilliant young man who was honest, hard-working, and understanding, and one of the finest men I have ever worked with or for. He didn't play politics.

His organization (1,500 people or so) was doing an excellent job, and it showed. He always said our work, progress, and results speak for themselves and we don't have to advertise or play politics to get ahead.

When he missed out on a promotion to the next higher position, he resigned. Now, more than 15 years later, I see him occasionally. He has moved around to several smaller companies, but never got a second big chance. One wonders how much higher he could have gone if he had played politics to protect what he had.

Another situation involved a friend who had risen to a vice-presidency after 20 years with the same company. He was totally a company man, but he and the president had their disagreements, and opposing factions developed in the office.

Suddenly, at a board meeting one month, the president was given a new position on the board, and the leader of the opposition forces was voted in as president.

My friend resigned when he was asked to leave. His years of hard work, devotion, and performance meant nothing. At this writing, he is still not employed. He was done in by office politics.

Whether we like it or not, office politics can help us or hurt us, according to how we play. If you choose not to play, you do so at your own peril, because someone sooner or later will play the game to reach for what you want or have. You can lose by default just as easily as you can by playing and losing.

Several situations give rise to office politics:

1. A vacancy arises for a higher position in the company.

2. Your department or organization is doing well and growing rapidly.

3. Your department or organization is not doing well and a cutback, layoff, or reorganization is in the offing.

4. A new top manager arrives from outside to take over.

5. Your immediate supervisor is taking the credit for your work and the work of others, and he or she is holding you back from more rapid advancement.

6. Relatives or close personal friends of the boss are hired and/or promoted.

There are other situations from which politics will arise, but let's discuss how to handle these six situations.

When a higher position is available for which many are qualified and interested, politics really comes into play.

Standing aside from the competition and letting your performance and results speak for themselves usually doesn't ensure that the deserving will win the promotion.

When I worked for the government, I reported to a scientist who was in charge of three divisions, computers, communications, and engineering. My computer group was larger than the other two combined. We did our jobs well and let it go at that.

Occasionally, I would see the chief of communications going out to lunch with the technical director (my boss), but I thought little about it. My boss, who traveled frequently, appointed the chief of communications as acting tech director during his absence. During these periods, when I requested some direction or information from the acting tech director, I got either no reply or bad information.

When I heard that the chief scientist was leaving and my boss was up for the promotion, I asked him to consider me for his vacant position. My boss replied that during the past two years when he was traveling or on vacation, the chief of communications had run the entire group well and deserved the promotion. Now we were into the politics, and I decided to act. I asked if he knew what really went on during his absence. I explained many situations in which our group had to operate on its own, with no help or direction from anyone. He was surprised. The acting director wasn't directing us at all, but he told the boss he was. I explained that our computer group contained over 50% of the total staff, over 75% of the budget, and really produced the product.

After several more meetings and discussions, I received the promotion. I had to play politics to do it. You either participate or lose.

Remaining silent in such situations can work to your disadvantage. If you want the promotion, then ask for it, and convince the boss to at least listen to you. False modesty has cost many people further career advancements.

When your department is doing well or growing, there are opportunities for office politics of both a defensive and an offensive nature.

The best way to expand is "into the vacuum." That means go where nothing precedes you. In forming a new group or marketing a new product, you are unlikely to meet with much political resistance, because you are replacing or supplanting no one.

Defensive politics becomes necessary when some political empire builder sees opportunities for himself if he can gather you and your group under his control. It is a sign that someone wants you because you are doing a good job.

When our computer group grew and became very profitable, several empire builders tried to get the general manager to reorganize so that I would have to report to them. I had to constantly repel such attempts. My secretary became a valuable ally as my intelligence officer in this battle. On several occasions, my secretary advised me that at the next manager's meeting a certain individual was going to propose a reorganization that included transferring our department under his control, and I had better get ready to defend against it.

How did she find out? Her friend who worked in the typing pool had typed up the proposed new plan and had run off copies. Sometimes, I even got one in advance. I was not caught by surprise and could clearly refute or reject each point or argument presented at the meeting, because I was prepared.

Another ploy is to propose that you take over others' groups, before they get a chance to give their presentations. Even if you don't want it, bring it up for discussion first. They will be so preoccupied with arguments as to why the organization should stay as it is that they will never get around to presenting their new plan. Sometimes the best defense is a good offense.

If your group is not doing well, you are ripe for a political move against you, and you can easily lose on the basis of profit or loss numbers. The only way to prevent a takeover move from outside your group is to strike first.

Go to your boss, admit the problem, and ask for help if you need it. You are more likely to retain control this way, even if people are sent in to help turn it around. You are likely to stay in the saddle and have the newcomers assigned under your authority.

When a new boss arrives, things will change.

Don't wait to meet the new boss. Get your licks in first, because most people tend to believe what they hear first. Also, don't assume that they must know about you and your good work. Sometimes they don't unless you tell them.

When a boss continually takes credit for your work or holds you down, the only political maneuver open to you is the end run (see Chapter 9). This is a dangerous move and is seldom successful. It is best to quietly leave if you can.

In a situation involving close friends or relatives of the boss, no political action will work. Don't even try any. Your only choices are to accept it or leave.

Office politics may be distasteful, but the person interested in advancing as far as possible must learn to master it.

You will survive and prosper in the long run if the word gets around that in addition to your professional ability you are astute politically and can defend yourself and your organization. When people see you beat the politicians at their own game, and you outproduce them as well, then most of them will leave you alone and go after smaller fry.

25
Priorities

The heavens themselves, the planets and this centre
observe degree, priority, and place.
—*William Shakespeare*

As a person attains progressively higher positions, it naturally follows that his or her responsibilities become greater. The person has a wider range of things to do that can't be done in the same time or with the same efficiency.

One has to make several choices. First, what is most important? What is not? What has to be done first? Sometimes such routine matters as weekly reports or time cards must be submitted by a rigid time schedule. They aren't necessarily the most important things to do, but they can't be neglected either.

At the same time that this person takes on more responsibility and his job becomes more complex, he receives progressively less supervision or direction. As this starts to occur, in any person's career, he must set up a priority list of what to do and when. In setting up your priorities, you reveal a great deal about yourself. You indicate, for all to see, important facts about your work, yourself, and what you want to be. In some measure, you make the job what you want it to be by what you consider important and what you spend your time doing.

Consider the first-time manager who has responsibility over several people. The job is partly technical and partly managerial. No longer responsible for only himself, he must consider how to direct, motivate, and train other people to do the assigned task. For the first time he has a budget and a schedule to consider. He must apportion his time during the working day according to what he considers important. He must set up priorities. The best way is to write a list of all things to be done, rearrange them in order of importance, and change or modify the list daily, weekly, or whenever required.

If you create a priority list, discuss it with your boss, and get his or her comments or suggestions, you may be surprised to find that there are other matters you are supposed to attend to, or there are things on your list for which you aren't responsible. If you plunge ahead on your own and hope for the best, later events may reveal you left out an important item, or you spent an excessive amount of time on less important tasks, but you find out too late.

I chose this example of the first-time manager because it is at this stage that most fail, and progress up the corporate ladder stops or slows drastically. Consider the highly qualified technical or business person. After several years doing a progressively better job as a mathematician, accountant, chemist, or salesman, he gets promoted to his first manager's job. He now spends more time than ever doing his job even better. He wants to show appreciation for the promotion and higher salary by being more productive than ever. After all, that is why top management promoted him, right? *Wrong!*

As a manager with other responsibilities, a person is supposed to *direct* and *control* the action rather than be the most productive participant. But the person who tries to outperform all subordinates combined is so busy working extra hours that he gives little time and attention to training others, schedules, and costs. This can only lead to eventual failure when the project ends over budget or over schedule, or some subordinate resigns because his manager has no time for him, and there is no one trained and ready to take over that job.

Such people have a completely false or wrong set of priorities and work on the wrong job, doing the wrong thing, for the wrong reason, and end failing to manage. They did what they knew rather than knowing what to do.

Take time to write a priority list, check it out with the boss, revise it as the ebb and flow of daily action indicates, and keep your priorities straight and current.

First-time managers fail mostly by having a mixed-up priority list or none at all. If they do the first management task well, then most can progress to higher management ranks.

Nothing is ever exactly the same twice, so don't assume that your next or higher management job will be the same as that you have now and in which you perform so well.

Most senior managers are happy to advise and guide you upward. All you have to do is ask.

Recently, I read about a man who is president of one of the largest corporations in the world. His wife told the reporter that right after they were married her husband made a priority list and time schedule for his career advancement. They were both in their mid-twenties then. At the age of 35 his wife said he was two weeks off his schedule. He benefited from setting a priority list and was able to stick to it long enough to get where he wanted to be.

Look ahead five years or so. What do you want to be then? Set your priorities to get there, and do it.

26
Relatives at Work

It is a melancholy truth that even great men have their poor relations. —Charles Dickens

Relatives and work usually don't mix well. Most executives will tell you not to hire relatives or even do business with them; yet, most of them do so and freely admit it. (See the executive survey at the beginning of this book.)

During my career, I have had the experience of working with and observing the relatives of bosses and other co-workers. Many companies have explicit rules that forbid a husband-and-wife team at work. Mishandling an executive's son or daughter who is working for the summer can adversely affect any young manager, so let us discuss the pitfalls that can happen and how to handle them.

The boss comes in with his arm around a kid's shoulder and says to you, "This is my son. He is back from school and I want to give him one of those summer jobs we have every year." He goes on to say, "Don't give him any special consideration. Treat him just like the rest, and if he gets out of line, then discipline him just as you would anyone else."

Don't you believe it. This boy may have your future career in his hands, so be aware of it and act accordingly. Do all you can to help him along. Make him like you. It will be over in September anyway.

Remember, he lives with the boss, is deeply loved and admired by the boss, and talks to the boss at places and

157

times you can't. If the son says good things about you to the boss, all well and good. If reports are not favorable, this could be bad for you and others.

A manager brought his daughter in to work for the summer. The girl was a quiet, hard worker. Everyone knew who she was, but she settled into her job and was accepted. After a month or so, she was part of the group working in a backroom area. Everyone liked her and talked with her, and talked openly with others in her presence.

In all innocence, while driving home with her dad one evening, she told him what was going on in the backrooms. One thing he heard upset him. A secretary was fired, and a man severely disciplined, as the result of this conversation between the boss and his daughter.

We hired a senior scientist's younger brother for the summer to work on one of our jobs at a military installation. The boy's first infraction was putting up anti-war posters in the offices on the military post.

Late one afternoon, I got a call at our home office about ten miles from this base. The boy, dressed in old army dungarees and old army jacket, waited for the bus outside of the office, but still on the base. The base military police took one look at him and, quite naturally, concluded he was a serviceman who was out of uniform (no hat) and sloppily dressed. They asked to see his identification card. Instead of telling them he was a civilian working on the base, he gave vent to his anti-war protest, shouting "fascist pigs" and "war mongers." He was on his way to the stockade until some of our senior people heard the scuffle and intervened.

When I didn't take the boy's side in the matter, his older brother left our company. We lost the services of an excellent man, because I hired his kid brother for the summer.

You run a constant risk when you employ relatives. If

you ever have trouble with one relative, then, most likely, you will hear from the other one as well. It doesn't matter who is right or wrong.

If you are a senior executive, have some pity on your subordinates. When you bring in members of your family, you really place a burden on your people. Of course, they will smile at you and make the best of it, but they are afraid and will remain so until the relative leaves.

Hiring relatives for permanent positions is even worse. You may be in for a long and difficult period. If relatives work out badly, they can tell the boss that it is your fault. If they work out well, they could be promoted right over you.

It is possible that an executive's son who likes and respects you may put in a good word for you, but the opposite could happen just as easily. Never forget who they are and don't treat them the same as everyone else.

27
Resignations

We, in some unknown power's employ
Move on a rigorous line
Can neither, when we will, enjoy
Nor, when we will, resign.   —*Matthew Arnold*

Few people give much thought to resignations. The new job, the raise, and the promotion all deal with some sort of new beginning, whereas resignations deal with the end of something.

Resignations are an important part of one's career. It is a mistake to think that the old job, former bosses, and co-workers are of no further value to you in your future career.

Managers' most common criticisms about departing employees are the following:

1. Loss in interest in the current job and a decline in job performance before the resignation and during the notice period.

2. Sudden increase in the use of sick leave or absence from work during the notice period.

3. Late arrivals to work and/or early departures.

4. Disturbing other employees by unnecessary visits or chats.

5. Settling old scores around the office and "telling off" those who, for one reason or another, the departing employee never liked.

6. "Bad mouthing" the boss or the organization.

7. Sudden departure that leaves work undone and creates a temporary problem for the boss or company.

Problems created by departing employees are not uncommon. Among them are sudden changes in behavior patterns and work habits. Psychologists advise us that some people subconsciously create an argument or some problem at work in order to justify their decision to leave.

Two large commercial organizations have adopted strict policies concerning resignations. An employee who resigns is removed from the office or plant on the same day, if possible. The companies will pay departing employees for the period of notice they wish to give, but the policy is to remove them from their jobs immediately before they can cause departure problems. The policy also applies to managers.

If immediate removal is not possible and some work must be completed, then the departing person is isolated insofar as possible from contact with other employees.

Our company has this same policy now. It arose out of necessity, because of departure problems from people during their period of notice. The policy protects those who are leaving from making a mistake that can write off years of good work, and it protects the company and co-workers from problems the departing employee may create.

Here are some mistakes people make when resigning:

1. The person leaving mistakenly believes that he will never again need anything from the place he leaves.

You may need references if and when you move again to another job. The next place may want references from each former place of employment listed on your résumé.

2. The person leaving mistakenly believes that he or she will never again meet or come into business contact with former bosses, co-workers, or subordinates.

You may keep "running into" people from your former

place of employment. Bosses and managers move around too.

3. The person leaving may not consider that he or she may want to rejoin the company later on. A sizable minority of people who resign eventually choose to come back later, or at least try to return.

4. The person uses the resignation as an instrument to gain something from his current employer. This is a form of blackmail.

Don't ever submit a resignation unless you really intend to leave. If your superiors suddenly become aware of your value as you prepare to leave, let them approach you.

If people find that a resignation will get them an early or extra-generous raise, the word gets around, and management is buried in threatened resignations.

If you leave with bad feelings, you cut off forever the opportunity to come back. One never knows what the future will bring.

Some years ago, one of our managers had an excellent secretary. She worked well for him for more than four years. One day, the boss heard a rumor at the coffee machine that she was going to resign because of pregnancy.

The manager was offended that she did not tell him first. Moreover, during the ensuing month, her attitude changed abruptly. She came into work late, left her desk during the day to roam the office, and departed early in the afternoon. Before the month was up, her boss asked her to leave and had her paid off to the end of the month.

Five years later, when her child was in kindergarten, she reapplied for employment. Although her former boss was no longer there, the exit interview that most personnel departments require was in the files. One question had the wrong answer. It was, "Do you recommend she be rehired?" The file report contained a negative reply and described her behavior just prior to her departure. She was not rehired.

Here's a list of what to do and not to do when you consider resigning:

1. Tell your immediate supervisor first and no one else if he or she wants it that way.

2. Arrange a mutually convenient departure date (two to four weeks usually). Do not leave suddenly or with your work undone.

3. In your written resignation, say something nice about your boss and co-workers. They will like this and will remember it. Say you learned a lot or it was pleasant to work with such nice people. This goes in your file, and you may want a recommendation or to return someday. Look ahead to future possibilities.

4. Wish everyone well.

5. Don't complain or criticize anyone. If you put up with it while you worked there, you can tolerate it for a few more weeks.

6. Maintain good work habits.

7. Don't use up your sick leave before you go. It leaves a bad impression.

8. Don't submit a resignation unless you really intend to leave.

9. It is best to leave on a friendly basis. If you had difficulties with anyone during your time with the company, seek the person out, patch it up before you leave, and shake hands. It won't hurt and could help you later on.

10. Before you resign from one position, make sure that you are completely set for the new position. If your new place of employment requires a physical examination in order to work there (many companies require this today for group insurance purposes and other reasons), be sure you take and pass the physical before you resign.

A man who resigned from the place where I worked left on a Friday with a farewell luncheon, a gift, and everyone's best wishes. On Monday, he reported for work at his new company. When he took the "routine" physical, it was discovered he had a serious illness of which he had been unaware. The company didn't hire him and our company, having learned about his illness, wouldn't take him back either.

The man's medical and life insurance premiums had been a company-paid fringe benefit. He could have kept the policies after 30 days by paying on his own, but, with no job, he couldn't afford the high individual premiums.

If he had taken the physical before he resigned, at least he could have remained at his old job for a while and be covered by the medical plan and the company-paid insurance policy. We heard that he died a year or two later with no life insurance for his widow and children.

In summary, when resigning, keep in mind that this phase of your career will have a carryover into the future. Your contact with the organization is not over, and later you may need a reference, or meet the same people again as co-workers or superiors. Don't burn your bridges, because you may also want to return.

28
Responsive People

Good the more communicated more abundant grows.
—John Milton

Responsiveness is a desirable characteristic. A responsive person is not necessarily a "yes man" or someone who does what he is told in a thoughtless manner. The responsive person reacts, and the reaction or response is visible and easy to understand. People may agree or disagree, but they respond, and others find them easy to work with or anticipate.

The responsive person shows how he or she feels about an idea, proposal, or suggestion, and usually shows enthusiasm as well. Most of us need visible reactions to our working efforts and ideas from time to time. You may not always like the response, but you will know where you stand.

Why are so many people we meet at work unresponsive? They show little or no reaction to whatever they are told to do. New ideas and techniques are received with a "loud clap of silence."

There persists in business and elsewhere a school of thought that says always "keep your cool"; never let anyone know what is really on your mind or how you really feel; don't commit yourself to anything; don't get involved.

When senior managers or staff give presentations or talks to juniors, there often is little reaction. Some people are afraid to disagree or to ask questions that the boss may not be able to answer. Even when the boss asks each one individually how he or she feels about the subject, others remain unresponsive.

If you really want true reactions or response, ask for written, unsigned questions or comments and collect them so no one can be identified as the author of any question.

If you correspond with someone (don't do this to supervisors; they don't like it) who doesn't reply, prepare in your next communication some action item and state that the action will take place or the decision will take effect on or after a given date.

Next, state in your memo or letter that you realize the recipient is busy, so no response is necessary unless he or she disagrees. Now, no response has been converted in your letter or memo into agreement or consent as soon as the five-day response limit passes.

Responses and participation are stimulated by such memos. People won't like it or possibly even you, because you are forcing them to respond when they don't want to, but it is a good method to get reactions or to move ahead on some task that requires action from a number of people who never seem to be available.

Sometimes you must develop techniques to stimulate a response from a client who is uncommunicative. You can't order a response from anyone, but you can set up a situation in which a person wants to respond.

You can request, even demand, response from subordinates, but that is difficult with a boss whose nature is to be withdrawn, unenthusiastic, and nonresponsive.

You can openly discuss the situation with your boss and explain how difficult it is when he exhibits little or no reaction to your ideas or suggestions. Some bosses may then make an effort to be more responsive. Others may figure it is your place to adjust to their personalities. You may succeed where all else fails if you develop a technique of crediting ideas to the boss as if they originated with him.

In summary, responsiveness is best when it is spontaneous, but it can be stimulated if you develop some techniques. Never try to use exactly the same methods in the same way again, because people and circumstances change from time to time and place to place.

29
Socializing at Work

The social smile; the sympathetic tear. . . .
—*Thomas Gray*

The workplace has become a major source of social relationships in today's mobile society. No longer does the family remain fixed near the place of birth. The extended family of aunts, uncles, and cousins living in the same town, and grandparents in the same house or just down the street, is disappearing. Today a child grows up, goes away to school, and finds a job in another city some distance from the homestead. As a result, the large family group as a center of social activity is becoming rare.

Also, the church is no longer the source of close social activity. The local clergyman once knew your grandparents and your parents and probably baptized you and watched you grow up. Clergy visits to one's home were commonplace. The church was the center of much social activity in addition to religious services.

As people, especially the younger ones, are now less influenced by traditional religion, another social outlet is becoming less available to them.

This leaves work as the third major source of social activity. The job is the only opportunity for many to meet other people, get to know and like them, and develop social relationships. Many large companies, aware of this need, sponsor at some expense such social activities as softball and bowling leagues, golf, tennis, and bridge clubs for employees.

Sometimes these relationships lead to romance and marriage, or romance, divorce, and remarriage. But here we are discussing the kind of social affiliation or friendship that develops between two or more people who work at similar jobs, share common interests, have some common likes and dislikes, have similar educational or cultural backgrounds, and have similar career goals.

With the diminished role of extended family and church as sources of social relationships, the work-related social relationship becomes important. When most people are asked, "What is your primary reason for working?" they usually reply, "To make a living." However, a deeper analysis indicates that money is not the sole or primary reason for working. There are many others.

Surveys indicate a difference in the reasons for working between high-paid personnel ($50,000 a year and up) and the majority who earn far less. The lower-paid group listed reasons for working in this order: full appreciation of work performed; sympathetic help on personal problems; feeling "in" on things. This group listed "good pay" fifth. The higher-paid group, when asked their order of priorities for working, replied as follows: good pay; job security; promotion and growth (opportunity for more pay). This group listed at the bottom the three reasons that the lower-paid group gave top priority.

Top wage earners seem to work for highly personal reasons, and those in the lower salary range tend to work for more social reasons. As careers unfold and time goes on, each group gets what it really wants. The highly paid executives pursue and make more money. That is their top priority item, and it comes first for them with most everything they do. The more socially oriented people make more friends, develop and maintain great working relationships, but earn less money.

This is not to say that one set of goals is right and the other wrong. All of us make up our own minds about what we want from a working career. Be aware, however, that if you opt for working primarily for social reasons, then you are less likely to earn a great deal of money. You don't think earning money is really that important. This attitude will be shown throughout your entire working career and permeate your decisions, your work habits, and your behavior to such an extent that you may turn down an opportunity for a transfer to a better-paying job or a promotion to higher management.

It is understandable in today's world that most people socialize around and through the place they work because the home, neighborhood, and church social outlets are no longer available to the same extent they were in the past. You should be aware, though, if you put social reasons first and income lower in priority, this will have a negative effect on your potential earning capacity. It all depends on what you want.

Let me cite an example. We promoted one of our technical staff to his first manager's position. He was responsible for the work of five people in addition to his own work. He became very protective of "his" people.

The manager did the work for "his" people, covered up for their mistakes, and helped them far too much. A close bond of "us" against "them" developed, wherein he became sort of a father figure who was always there to help and support them. As a result, false progress reports were submitted to higher management. Each member of his group became isolated from the overall project and company goals. Social relationships had taken over.

Be aware, then, that in the long run most of us will get from our careers just about what we want or are willing to accept. Those who strive for and reach the top (or near to the top) of their chosen profession are not always the smartest or the luckiest. They have highly personal career plans and goals. They use their careers to earn the income necessary to reach their goals and they socialize, in general, with a different group from those with whom they work. They realize that close personal associations at work probably will conflict with their career goals, so they avoid developing such relationships.

It is not unusual to find executives in one company socializing with their counterparts in other companies (lawyers, doctors, CPA's, vice-presidents, or company presidents). They sometimes find they have much more in common with these executives than with the ones in their own organizations.

The "socializers" at work tend not to reach the higher levels in their chosen professions because career advancement is not their first priority. They spend time and energy on others. This is what they want to do. It becomes their reward, so they seek it out constantly.

You can't mix the two approaches, because at times they will conflict. Going to the extreme in either situation is wrong. The hard-driving executive who pursues his career goals to the exclusion of friendship, family life, or anything else usually ends up wealthy, divorced, and alone. The person who spends his time at work constantly helping others, socializing, and advancing others' careers is popular but broke.

Finally, do not confuse friendship with shared common interests. True friendship stands the test of time and separation, and grows. Shared common interests do not. At the time, it is easy to confuse one with the other.

As people move from one job to another, they usually exchange one set of co-workers for another, and in time social contacts with former co-workers become more infrequent because their interests are no longer the same. But true friendships survive.

30
Staff Positions

Stay close to your desk and never go to sea; and you all
may be rulers of the Queen's Navee.
—*Gilbert & Sullivan,* H.M.S. Pinafore

In any business organization, jobs fall into two general
categories, line functions and staff functions.

Line functions have to do with the performance of a
particular task or contract. Examples are engineering,
manufacturing, and production. Staff functions are support units such as accounting, personnel, legal, payroll,
advertising, and quality assurance. Line functions are
called direct work in that the work is directly related and
charged to a client, contract, or customer. Staff functions
are sometimes called indirect work because their charges
come under overhead or general and administrative expenses.

People can choose some fine careers in either line, but is
one preferable to the other if you aim for the top? I believe
the line function is the place for you if you aspire to top
management. People who can earn money for the company are looked upon most favorably by higher management.

In my experience, some staff people consider themselves a "cut above" the line people, factory workers, or
those who work directly for the client. They work in
cleaner surroundings and come in the same front door as
the corporate officers.

However, when a recession hits or sales decline, the first order of company business is the lowering of overhead, and staff or support personnel are laid off. At the same time, other employees may be working overtime to complete a line project on schedule.

What does this all mean to the aspiring young professional? In my opinion, you have a greater probability of reaching higher up the ladder if you are able to operate and manage a line organization rather than be a staff person.

With the recent and welcome emergence of women into the professional ranks in greater numbers, more women will find their way up the corporate ladders. This is great and overdue. A woman executive recently issued a warning to professional women. She noted that they were going into staff or overhead positions in disproportionate numbers to those entering line positions. She noted that most top professionals in organizations come from the line, not the staff. She suggested that women were going into dead-end positions from which, at some point later in their careers, further advancement will not be possible. How far can the head of personnel, or the payroll manager, or a staff assistant to the general manager go? How far can the manager of a successful and profitable project go?

In some situations, going on staff can broaden your knowledge and experience in that you gain exposure across the board and learn how the organization works as a whole. In many staff positions, however, you don't make decisions. You make recommendations to others who make the decisions. You will never get to the top in any career unless you are willing and able to make decisions, and that takes practice. If you spend a lot of your time and career on staff to some higher authority, you may find that you seldom, if ever, get an opportunity to make decisions.

If you are offered a staff position in early or mid-career,

I recommend that you look at it carefully before you take it. The immediate benefits are obvious. You meet people who can help you later in your career, if they get to know and like you. You are near the trappings of power and authority, but remember, your value may exist only in your service and importance to another individual rather than in your own ability and experience.

A close personal friend of mine, who worked for more than 20 years for the same company, rose to staff assistant to the company president, and was happy with his job. He was hard-working, competent, and very close to the company president. It all disappeared quickly for him when the company president was moved up to the board of directors. In came a new president, out went the old president's staff, my friend included, and in came a new staff. This experience is not unusual for those in staff positions.

When times are good and overhead money is in plentiful supply, executives and senior managers gather more people around them. When there is a downturn in business, this staff will suddenly be cut back, and administrative assistants and senior staff consultants find their positions disappear.

So look carefully at those staff assignments before you take one, because they can shunt you aside in mid-career, and you may have some difficulty in returning to the mainstream later on.

Index